About the Authors

The life of a musician can be exhilarating, but it can also be tough. Ann Cherry and Robert Hawkins share some of their best, as well as their worst, experiences with us. Ann was born into a musical family; a talented youngster, she attended the Manhattan School of Music in New York and the Royal Academy of Music in London. Her professional career spanned orchestral playing, chamber groups and solo work. She has appeared on radio and television in many countries. Bob was born into the life of the Methodist church. With a career as a Methodist Minister which moved him around the State of Virginia at regular intervals, he had to indulge his love for music-making anywhere and in any way he could. His first instrument was the trumpet, followed closely by clarinet, recorder and finally the flute. He played with several bands and renowned musicians over the years. Today Bob has severe arthritis and Ann has Parkinson's disease. Both have, very reluctantly, finally put down their instruments. Now Ann and Bob have begun a new chapter in their lives: the search for health. Robert has remained conventional in his approach, whereas Ann is researching alternative therapies.

Why Did This Happen To Me?
... Is inspirational.

Why Did This Happen To Me?

By Ann Cherry & Robert Hawkins

Why Did This Happen To Me?

Vanguard Press

VANGUARD PAPERBACK

© Copyright 2010
Ann Cherry & Robert Hawkins

The right of Ann Cherry & Robert Hawkins
to be identified as authors of
this work has been asserted by them in accordance with the
Copyright, Designs and Patents Act 1988.

All Rights Reserved

No reproduction, copy or transmission of this publication
may be made without written permission.
No paragraph of this publication may be reproduced,
copied or transmitted save with the written permission of the publisher,
or in accordance with the provisions
of the Copyright Act 1956 (as amended).

Any person who commits any unauthorised act in relation to
this publication may be liable to criminal
prosecution and civil claims for damages.

A CIP catalogue record for this title is
available from the British Library.

ISBN 9781843866022

Vanguard Press is an imprint of
Pegasus Elliot MacKenzie Publishers Ltd.
www.pegasuspublishers.com

First Published in 2010

Vanguard Press
Sheraton House Castle Park
Cambridge England

Printed & Bound in Great Britain

Acknowledgements

Ann says:

A big thank you to my husband Paul Rodriguez for his patience and encouragement as well as helping me to use a computer.

Thanks also Timothy Morris (kinesiologist) and George Topping (hypnotherapist) – two amazing people interested in alternative therapies.

Robert says:

Thank you to Thomas J. Hawkins - my father, mentor and best friend who taught me the meaning of "loving the unlovable".

Bishop Kenneth Goodson - Virginia Conference of the United Methodist Church; Presiding Bishop, deceased. For not charging me with heresy and high crimes against the Church.

Milton Cherry - Guided, encouraged and inspired me through example and instilled in me his love of great music.

Dedication

This book is dedicated to those who are battling against incurable disease.

Chapter 1 (Ann)

(1943 – 1963)

The year was 1943. I was born in Baton Rouge, Louisiana, into a musically snobbish but financially challenged family. My parents both played the violin and loved nothing on earth as much as the Beethoven string quartets. Mother was a pupil of my father until they got married, and then she taught him how to play. Music was the name of the game and Beethoven, with Bach a close contender, led the field.

My father's first professional job was as assistant concertmaster in the New Orleans Philharmonic, and he taught at Louisiana State University (where my mother was his student). My older brother and sister, like me, were born in the Deep South. The summer I turned three we moved to Ithaca. Ithaca (named for the Greek island) is in central New York State. I think Daddy felt that New York would provide more musical opportunities than Louisiana. I also think he later regretted this decision for family reasons.

When Daddy taught at Ithaca College of Music, he and Mother formed the Cherry String Quartet. I think they must have been pretty good because they seemed always to be giving concerts. But times were hard for everyone in those years, and we lived in a small flat above a grocery store. There were lots of bugs! Mother took in typing to earn a few extra pennies. Mother was constantly saying to me, "Sit still, Ann, and be quiet!" – two dictums pretty hard for a preschooler. The area we lived in was rough and apparently all three of us kids were growing up to be hoodlums. My memories of the years in Ithaca are not pleasant ones. I remember being chased in front of a car by a boy a bit older than I who was wielding a knife. Fortunately, the driver managed to stop in time, but the boy ran away before anyone could catch him. I remember seeing my older sister in a nasty gang fight. She was known as Queen of the Alley Cats and the opposing gang leader was dubbed (by my sister, I think) as Queen of the Trash Cans. It sounds silly, but the fighting was real – head banging on concrete kerbs and stone throwing. My brother, the nicest of the three of us, met a young girl who was pregnant – not by him (he was twelve), but he wanted to help her anyway by marrying her. He felt hurt when Mother and Dad refused to give permission, but I seriously doubt that the girl would really have wanted a husband quite so young!

I did come up with a useful scheme to help financially, but my parents quickly put an end to it. I stood on the street corner and offered to passers-by, "Will you swap your money for mine?" My money was monopoly money. I was doing quite well until somebody told on me!

The school I attended was a large, old and imposing building with a baseball diamond between the swings and the entrance – not the cleverest arrangement because, when the bell rang, the younger pupils had to run around the playing field. One day, in a hurry to get into the school, I cut corners and ran too close to the batter just as he swung the bat over his shoulder. Wallop! He caught me smack on the forehead. Apparently, I lost consciousness now and again, but I remember my father coming to take me to a nearby doctor. I don't know why I was taken there instead of to a hospital.

Because we were all growing up so badly, my parents decided that Daddy should accept a job offer from Richmond Professional Institute, in Virginia. They thought the South was more civilized. This was a career step backwards for my father and I'm quite sure he would not have accepted the position if he had not had children. Musically, Ithaca was much more lively.

The first year we lived in Richmond – I was now seven – we rented an old house, one of three on a largish farm ('Brookberry') just outside the city. We were lucky – our house had an indoor bathroom. There was an old cherry tree that I used to climb, sharing cherries with the bugs and little green worms. Ugh, I wouldn't do it now! Behind the house were lots of trees – I remember it as a small forest, but that's probably because I was young – where we three used to play. Well, not so much my brother, Mike; he was older and had his own set of friends. Anyway, that's how I came to be bitten by an infected tick and nearly died. I remember, when the fever was raging, that I was enjoying the special attention being given to me and I begged my parents, "Let's play cowboys and Indians." I was told to lie still. When the fever rose even more, I wanted to go to sleep and no one would let me. I remember Daddy carrying me to the car to take me to the hospital, and I don't remember any more about it until I was better. In spite of catching Rocky Mountain Spotted Fever (that's what the hospital thought I had, although there was no rash), I thoroughly enjoyed living on a farm. I got to know my brother better, and my sister and I used to huddle under a blanket after school and listen to *Sergeant Preston of the Yukon* and *The Shadow* on the radio until our parents returned from work and put on some heating. I thought that it was wonderful to have an older sister. No doubt my sister, on the other hand, often found me an encumbrance!

Oh, a little story from the Brookberry year comes to mind: one day my school held a fete and our dog must have sensed the extra excitement in the air. He followed Mary Grey (my sister) and me to the bus stop and when we wouldn't let him on the school bus, he calmly waited for the next one. He managed to get to the school and make his way to the hotdog stand. My sister and I were sent home with the dog.

We lived for only one year at Brookberry Farm, then we moved to a rented house on a quite wide and busy street and with a very small garden, where we also stayed for only a year. That was the year I ran away from home after a disagreement with my sister. When they returned from work and found me gone, my parents calmly made their way to the Colonial Supermarket's book section, where I was deeply ensconced in Jane and Peter's doggy adventures, and took me home. Not a word was said about my leaving home.

All this moving was hard on us children. I attended kindergarten and the first grade in Ithaca (where I was taunted mercilessly for having a Southern drawl), the second grade at a school near the farm in greater Richmond (where I was equally taunted for sounding like a Yankee!), the third grade in the city (where I had the most wonderful teacher in the world – aptly named Mrs. Loving), and the fourth until junior high at a school in Chesterfield County, which I didn't like much and which was academically below par. The constant moving was hard on all of us, but it was hardest on my brother who was a teenager; he kept losing his friendships. Well, we all suffered from the insecurity of not having a stable home life; I was sickly shy and I wet the bed until I was twelve. You would expect that we children would become closer than usual under these circumstances, but that's not the way it was. My brother kept more and more to himself as he got older, and the rivalry between my sister and me was rampant. She even accused me of killing the cat. Which I did not!

But for Mother and Dad things seemed, at last, to be going right. When I was nine they bought their first house. This is where I really remember the music. Occasionally their string quartet – now named the Richmond String Quartet – rehearsed at home. I always listened until I was sent to bed. They played a regular series of concerts at the Virginia Museum. I think at one time they actually had a cellist they liked, but most of them must have been pretty dire. I remember Mother telling about a time when they were playing a movement (probably Beethoven) with a fugal entrance, the cellist last. And he missed his entry. All my mother could think was, "Thank God – no cello!"

There were also problems finding a good violist, so my mother changed to viola. She swore she never could read the clef, that she played the music by transposition. She really did have an incredible mind and ear.

Aside from one brief love affair with geometry and algebra, I always wanted to be a musician. I'm afraid, however, that I had absolutely no talent for the violin. I loved all the quartet rehearsals which my parents held at home, but I could never understand why, when I drew my cheap bow across my pint-sized fiddle, it didn't sound as nice as when my father drew his Hill & Son bow across his JB Guadagnini. My father was disappointed when I quit violin, and he didn't understand why I wanted to stop the lessons. Looking back, I don't suppose I ever told him it was the dreadful noise I made that was the problem. Perhaps that was also the reason my sister gave up violin before me, and my brother before her.

When my school began a wind band, I felt that, as I came from a musical family, I ought to take part in this new musical experience. My friends all played clarinet so I wanted to play clarinet too, but my mother refused to buy or rent one for me. She said to me, "Borrow your brother's flute." This was an old and barely functional instrument, though I didn't know that at the time, which my brother had found in a junk shop. At the time I thought Mom was mean, but now I can see how much money she must have spent giving her three children a grounding in music, only to see two of them toss that experience to the wind.

With the help of the bandmaster, William Troxell, and a fingering chart, I began to teach myself the flute. It wasn't long before I fell in love with the instrument. I have to admit, though, that my primary stimulus to study music was utterly selfish. It was a means of getting attention from very busy parents. I, and no doubt my sister and brother as well, frequently felt ignored.

Oddly enough, six months later when I went to junior high, I was put into the first band rather than the second or third. I suppose that was because of my musical background. I was last chair of five flute players, but I was badly bitten by the music bug and I also experienced my first taste of competitiveness. By the next year I had moved up to second chair and then finally to first position. The boy who had been first chair quit the band rather than lose his position to me, and I am embarrassed now by my callousness when I remember how hurt he was. But I got better marks than he in the All-State competitions, and I also won first chair in the All-State concert band. My mother often said to me in later years that if there had been no concert band in my high school, I would never have attended school at all. She was right about that! By the way, I'm still in contact with the boy – a grandfather now – who played principal clarinet at All-State that year. He chose to become an enthusiast rather than a performer.

I begged my parents for flute lessons; I had dropped both piano and violin lessons, so flute lessons were given to me as a birthday present, which meant I was morally obligated to continue taking them, no matter what. At the first lesson I was so excited that I could hardly contain myself. I said to my teacher, "I want to learn to tongue and to play with vibrato!" and she replied in a most quelling manner, "I know what you need." So much for encouragement and enthusiasm! I hated those lessons after that. But I went to them – I was obliged to – and to give her credit, my teacher did teach me articulation.

This same teacher entered me, at the age of sixteen, in a concerto competition playing the Ibert Flute Concerto. It was far too hard for me. I was also playing the Haydn Concerto, but she entered me on the Ibert. I made a mess of it, of course. She also never tried to correct my hand position. I was double-jointed and held the flute in the most appalling way! In fact, I had to move to London before I studied with a teacher with the foresight to see that what I was doing to my fingers might lead to serious problems in the future.

My last year of high school – I skipped a year by attending summer school regularly and building up enough credits to get out early – I also played in the Richmond Symphony. I didn't really enjoy it much. It was all evening work and I had to do homework. I remember one night when a woman in the orchestra, who was to drive me home, decided for some reason not to take me all the way. She left me near a phone box on Hull Street – not the greatest area of town! – and I had to phone my father to come and get me. He was angry. I thought at the time he was angry with me, but as I got older I realized he was angry with the woman for leaving me alone in such a rough area.

One day I decided – spurred by my mother – that I should write a letter to William Kincaid, principal flute of the Philadelphia Orchestra, to ask him if he would give me lessons. I wrote a voluminous handwritten letter all about myself, most of which, I realized later, he did not read. I can't say I blame him! But he did write back and suggest that I telephone him to arrange a time for a consultation lesson. Now, here's the picture: my mother, sister and I sitting around the kitchen table staring at the phone, each trying to talk the other into making the call to the greatest flute player in the world. Finally, much to our surprise, my sister said, "I'll do it!" We handed her the telephone with great alacrity. She dialled. Kincaid answered. My sister thrust the phone at my unsuspecting mother and darted out of reach. I doubled over in laughter. Kincaid must have thought we were totally nuts, but my mother managed to arrange a time for the lesson.

My father drove me to Philadelphia. It was a beautiful morning and I just knew it was going to turn out to be a special day. Kincaid let me play to the bottom of the first page of the Haydn Concerto, and then asked me to sing the next passage without looking at the music. At the end of the audition he turned to my Dad and said, "I like what I hear." Daddy was so proud of me! He quoted that comment for years to come. I had a wonderful time that summer studying in Maine, sharing the top of a house across the lake from Kincaid's summer home with other flute pupils. Kincaid never allowed a cat in his garden, and birds and squirrels seemed to know it was a safe place. While I was sitting outside waiting for my lesson, the birds would sit on my shoulder and the squirrels would scamper across my feet. No exaggeration!

There was only one snag to this blissful picture, and that was telling my first teacher that Kincaid had accepted me as his student. I had decided not to let her know I was auditioning for Kincaid in case she insisted I play the Ibert Concerto. She was justifiably angry. But hell, she was quite young herself; she might have taken pride in the fact that one of her pupils had had some success.

My parents kept me at home for the year after I graduated from high school. They felt I needed to know some harmony and general musicianship before going to a conservatory, and they also felt I was too young to go away. They were absolutely right on both accounts! Clenching the matter was the fact that they would have been financially stretched to send me to a music conservatory while my sister was still at university (she too had skipped a year of high school). So, I studied harmony with my father at Richmond Professional Institute and took courses in music history and ear-training. My father also gave me flute lessons. Yes, he was a fiddle player, not a flautist, but he was also a fine musician. He thought my dynamic range needed improvement and he taught me to blow the Sevcik violin exercises as loud as possible. He had to keep a chair handy for when I got dizzy (he couldn't tell me about proper breathing, I had to figure that out by myself), but he did me a lot of good. It's a shame he didn't know enough about the technical aspects of flute playing to work on my clumsy hands!

Kincaid had agreed to accept me as his pupil at the Manhattan School of Music, but I still had to get through the entrance audition. My father took me from Richmond to New York and sat in the foyer while I was sent to this room and that one to complete different exams. I was in the middle of a music theory paper, sweating over what on earth an Alberti bass was, when I was called out for a sight-singing test. On my way back to the theory exam I saw my father sitting patiently and I thought, "Here's my salvation!" Grabbing the moment, I hurriedly asked him what this bass line was. Really, it's quite interesting: probably the only reason Domenico Alberti is remembered today is because of his harpsichord sonatas in which he consistently used a bass line of arpeggiated chords, always in the same pattern of lowest, highest, middle, highest. This was undoubtedly a technique already in practice, but Alberti was the first to make such extensive use of it.

I hated New York City. I was a Southern gal and I spoke with a slow drawl. New Yorkers didn't seem to have time to speak clearly, and I soon gave up trying to take a bus to school. I'd ask the driver, "Do y'all go to such-and-such a street?" and he'd reply so quickly that I hadn't a clue what he'd said. I'd answer, "Thank y'all," and get off. I got plenty of exercise, walking from the girls' hotel where I lived (78th Street) to the school in Upper Manhattan!

The girls' hotel where I lived was divided into two halves, expensive and not-quite-so-expensive. I lived in the latter section, which meant I shared a small room with someone else not of my choosing. My roommate was in New York to find a husband; she was twenty-five and beginning to feel desperate. I, being eighteen and having no finer feelings, used to tease her about this. Well, it was irresistible: every day she'd spend ages looking in the mirror and talking to her reflection. "Oh, Trudel," (her pet name for herself), "you're so clever!" she'd say, or similar things that showed her satisfaction with herself. I laughed. I shouldn't have laughed, I know; it was rude of me – and it made her determined to get rid of her childish roommate. She started telling me things like, "You're so unhappy, you're going to kill yourself." Every day she said that to me, for three solid months. Over and over. It was evil of her.

And that wasn't the only problem with the hotel. I couldn't eat the food. When I did, I inevitably vomited. So I lost weight and energy. As I was saving the bus fare by walking to school, I began spending my daily bus money (40 cents) on a cheese sandwich and a coke at a nearby delicatessen. The people running the deli must have realized that was all I was eating and my sandwiches got thicker and thicker. That was unbelievably nice of them! I take back my earlier comment. Some – most – New Yorkers are wonderful people!

Another problem I had with the hotel was practising. There was practice space in the basement, but you had to go outside and in again. There were windows high up the wall, at foot level to people on the street, and there was always some nutter looking in and making lewd comments.

My lessons with Kincaid were fortnightly. He'd had a heart attack by that time, but he was still an amazing teacher. A truly great man who lived for his music. I liked the Manhattan School of Music well enough, and I adored Kincaid; but I was lonely. The students lived all over the place and I didn't meet many people to socialize with, not even to go to concerts. When the Cleveland Symphony Orchestra came to Carnegie Hall, I went to meet Maurice Sharp, the principal flautist. We'd had some correspondence and I decided to leave New York and give life in Cleveland a whirl. I rationalized this by convincing myself that my parents were spending an awful lot of money keeping me in New York and I wasn't getting the practice to merit it. The naked truth is, I was miserable there.

The Cleveland Institute was much more enjoyable to me than the Manhattan School of Music. It is one of a group of five higher education institutions, all reasonably close to each other. I don't think I can name all five anymore: The Cleveland Institute of Music; Western Reserve University; a teaching hospital (Lakeside, one of the best hospitals in the USA); a nursing school; and Case Institute of Technology. Ha! I remembered all but one of the names! We all shared the same student union building, so there was a breath of sanity –

not the claustrophobia you can get from associating only with musicians!

I auditioned for a scholarship and received one offered by the Music and Drama Club of Cleveland. This club was good to me – they later partially funded my Wigmore Hall debut in London. And the entrance audition was much friendlier here. I had learned – memorized – a little Beethoven piano sonata and the school thought I could really play the piano; they put me into an advanced keyboard harmony group. Was that ever a mistake! I memorized the sonata because I had to watch my hands, not because I was fluent with the piece. And, it was the only piano work I could play. I struggled with keyboard harmony and passed only because one teacher realized my future would never depend on my piano playing, and he let me know in advance what was going to be on the exams.

The first year there I lived in the dormitory, and I had a lovely roommate, a nursing student. I got to know the caretaker of the CIM and he would let me and one or two others into the school when he arrived at 6am. I was able to get in two hours of practice before breakfast. I aimed for six to eight hours a day. What a pity that I still didn't know how to practise properly!

I ushered for Severance Hall, the home of the Cleveland Symphony. I heard the orchestra for free twice a week and I was actually paid to usher for the children's concerts! I also heard some other rather amazing concerts, including some jazz.

Mo Sharp would occasionally stop by the Institute between orchestra rehearsals, and when he did, he usually looked for me in the practice rooms and would give me an extra lesson. I had everything going for me except the school orchestra. The conductor, a real dodo, decided he didn't like me – this was before he even heard me play (and before he changed his mind enough to make a pass at me), and he told me that as a new student and a nobody, I had to watch the rehearsals rather than take part. He had no problem allowing another new student to play! Sharp looked in on the rehearsal one day and saw me sitting in the audience, and I gather he had a word with the conductor. At the next rehearsal I was allowed to sit in (last chair). They were playing Beethoven's third and when the orchestra reached that difficult flute solo in the last movement, the postgraduate student sitting first chair couldn't play it. The conductor stopped the orchestra and asked her if it was too hard for her.

"It's too hard for anyone," she responded. He then turned to me and asked:

"Can you play it?"

"I'll try," I replied, and he put down his baton, crossed his arms and told me to show him. So I did. I don't remember how accurate I was, but it must have been okay because I was moved up to principal flute. I also became principal flute in the opera orchestra and was invited to play a concerto with the percussion ensemble.

At this point I have to backtrack a little. The summer before my second year in Cleveland, I went to a music camp in North Carolina. There was a clarinettist there who was also on his way to the Cleveland Institute that autumn, and he apparently thought that gave him a right to hit on me. I didn't like him at all. I especially didn't like him because he frequently came into the breakfast room with his trousers undone, and I was usually the one elected to tell him. When I refused to go out with this creep, he spread the word around the camp that I was gay. In those days if you were homosexual you kept it to yourself; but anyway, I'm not gay.

Fortunately no one at the camp believed him. When the school term started at the Institute, there he was, once again pestering me to go out with him. He holds the honour of being the only man I ever tried to slap – and the bastard ducked! In the last term I became ill and was put in hospital for tests. There was nothing seriously wrong, but I was a little anaemic, had a little but constant temperature and I fainted a lot. I think I was exhausted more than anything. The school, however, was worried and suggested I take some time off, and my parents concurred. When I returned to Cleveland after a brief respite, I discovered that this same clarinettist had spread rumours to the effect that I had got pregnant. Again, I'm happy to say that no one really believed him. And then, fortunately for me, he found someone else to pester!

On November 22, 1963, President John F. Kennedy was assassinated in Dallas, Texas. I was sitting at my desk studying when my roommate was carried into our room.
"What's the matter with her?" I asked, unsympathetically.
"Haven't you heard about the President?" came the shocked reply.
"Of course," I said, returning to my books. I couldn't see that hysteria was going to help either Kennedy or me.

At Christmas time of my second year in Cleveland, I went with some friends to hear a jazz trumpeter playing at a black café. A lot of eyebrows shot up as we (all whities) walked in and it was a bit scary, especially as we went all the way to the back of the bar. No quick escape should we need it! Luckily the waitress was wonderful; she brought us paper hats and passed a cigar around which we all puffed, and then we were in with the crowd. The trumpeter was worth it. Sad to say, I can't remember his name.

However, a couple of months later I was not so lucky. I was run over by a hit-and-run driver. There was speculation that it was intentional; apparently a witness said the car picked up speed and headed for me deliberately, turning the car lights off so no one could read the licence number. At this time in the States (the early sixties), there were quite a few racial attacks. The driver was never caught. I spent two months in hospitals in Cleveland and then returned to Richmond for another eighteen months. My head had been split open, and although there was no permanent damage – thank God! – I had to learn to remember things again. I also had to have my two front teeth replaced. My two front teeth were the bane of my existence all my life. When I lost my baby teeth, the permanent teeth never came down. I went for a couple of years – no, longer – with no front teeth until my parents finally took me to a dentist and I had a bone, which was blocking them, cut away. If I never again hear the song about wanting two front teeth for Christmas, it will be too soon!

All this talk about teeth reminds me of what a dirty little scruff I was! One of my teachers in primary school kept pictures of her pupils pinned up on the wall. If your face and hands were clean, your photo was turned face up. My photo never faced the world. And the dentist used to have to remove the green mould from my teeth.

An aside: you know how many people who are seriously ill have a 'near death' experience? Well, I had one too, in the hospital, but it was very different from the norm. I dreamed that it was my decision whether to live or die (apparently that was true; the doctors told my parents it was up to me), and I wanted to know what death was like before I made a choice. So in my 'fantasy', I died. I don't know how long I was out, but eventually I woke up, aware that there had been nothing, and thinking to myself, 'The little bit of heaven on earth is worth all the hell on earth.' I remind myself of that even now, when the going gets rough.

I was with a friend the night of the accident, also a flautist. We were getting ready to move into a flat together and stopped off to buy some cleaning materials at a local shop. I can't remember anything after that, so this girl's story of what happened was crucial, both for me and for the police. My parents had a rider on their car insurance policy which covered any member of their family in any automobile accident, as long as it was not their fault. Apparently my friend came up with three different stories (I don't know in which order): the lights were in my favour; it all happened so fast she didn't know what the lights said; and finally, for the insurance adjuster, the lights were against me. I was told that the adjuster, who wanted to get the witness to say the accident was my fault, came away with a story about being invited into the kitchen for coffee – I gather that statement had implications – and finding another girl (my replacement) in bed with a boy. He felt her statement putting the blame on me was unreliable, and he advised the insurance company to make a generous settlement. Then the adjuster came to visit me in hospital and told me this girl was no friend of mine. She must have made quite an impression!

Here is a strange tale: about a week before the car incident, I began having a recurring dream. I was walking down a two-lane road, cars parked on both sides, and a dog with me. I was wearing a short, brown, suede jacket. As I approached the end of the road, I noticed that there was a flat-topped building on one corner and what seemed to be an open space in front of the building on the other side. I knew something was wrong. Then I woke up. I had this dream for about five nights in a row. And then it stopped.

In addition, I began receiving phone calls in the night; but when I answered there was only a dial tone. I heard knocking on the door, but when I opened it there was no one there. I heard knocking on the window – and again, no one was there. One night I sat up in bed and a figure was gesticulating to me.

"Tell me!" I demanded. And then the visions ceased.

Two nights later, I was wearing a brown, suede coat (knee length, not short as in the dream); I was on a two-lane road, cars on both sides. At the end of the street there was a flat-topped building on one side and a parking lot in front of a diner on the other. There was no dog with me, but the girl I was with made a pretty good metaphorical dog. At the corner I was hit by a car.

When I was back in Richmond, I went to a dentist who was wonderful and understood that my teeth needed to feel the same as the original ones. Coinciding with the arrival of my new teeth was a new flute. I had only the cheapest model student instrument at this point, really only suitable for beginners. The new silver Haynes flute helped me get my playing back to normal. I did try to finish my degree at the Cleveland Institute six months after the accident, but it was too soon and I had to drop out. Instead, I practised orchestral extracts and was offered a job with the Birmingham, Alabama, Symphony, which gave me the days free so I could complete my degree part-time.

Chapter 2 (Bob)

(1934 – 1953)

I was born October 6, 1934, in Richmond, Virginia, to my mother, a homemaker, and my father, a Methodist Minister. My earliest recollection is living in the parsonage of the Williamsburg Methodist Church. Our home was next door to a girls' dormitory at the College of William and Mary. I remember having babysitters from the girls' dorm when my parents went out. Even at such a young age, I was thrilled to have pretty girls take care of me in my parents' absence!

My father was appointed as the pastor of First Methodist Church in Norfolk, Virginia. This is where I started school. In spite of having a pastor for a father – or maybe because of it – I spent the first and second grades getting into trouble. The Second World War brought an early maturity to children. I did what I could to help Dad harvest vegetables in our Victory Garden. Food (especially sugar and butter) wasn't the only commodity rationed: gasoline, rubber (needed for automobile tyres), nylons and shoes come to mind, as well as the need to save metal clothes hangers.

To earn some extra money for myself as well as to help my family, I had a newspaper route. Every afternoon I rode my bicycle on my route delivering papers. Once a month I collected payments from my customers. This was a good job with a regular income, and I was grateful for it.

The war was in full swing. I can remember the fear caused by air raid drills in school. We students would go out into the hall, line both sides and kneel with our hands and arms covering our heads. One such drill was actually not a drill – it was the real thing. A German submarine was sighted off the Norfolk shoreline. This caused such intense fear among the local residents that you could taste it!

When I was in the third grade, we moved to Winchester, Virginia, where my father was sent to be the pastor of Braddock Street Methodist Church. He was gaining some recognition among his peers. Bishop Peal was our house guest once when I was about nine. To everyone's chagrin, I threw a snowball at him and hit Virginia's Episcopal leader squarely in the back of the head! The good man never complained. There was a public swimming pool in Winchester in those days. When I turned twelve, I passed the Red Cross Junior Life Course and was employed as a junior lifeguard at Willow Lawn Pool. I thoroughly enjoyed this summer in spite of discovering that the long hours in strong sunlight darkened my skin considerably.

It was in Winchester that I began my musical journey. Cornet lessons with Professor McAlwie and playing in the elementary school band are among my fondest memories of this period of my life. Aside from being kicked out of my Sunday School class for misbehaviour, and getting caught numerous times smoking, Winchester was a tranquil time in my young life. Would you believe it? Just as my brother Fred and I were getting accustomed to life in Winchester, word came from on high that we were moving to Danville, Virginia.

It seemed that God couldn't make up His mind where we were supposed to live! Little did I know then that this 'ecclesiastical chess game' was the way a talented and well-educated minister climbed the ladder of success. Evidently, my father was becoming successful. The church and the cities that we were located in grew bigger and bigger with each move. So did Dad's pay check!

It was in Danville that I really grew up. I fell in love for the first time (there were to be many more such times!) with a young lady named Sue; and I also fell in love with jazz (not necessarily in that order!). I started playing trumpet on weekends for dances. The various bands I played with travelled all over Virginia, North Carolina and even into West Virginia. These gigs were on weekends – I did little school homework. My high school education was sorely lacking; it just wasn't as exciting as my other interests!

Life in Danville and George Washington High School were some of the happiest days of my life. My younger brother, Fred, also counts these as the happiest, most carefree years he has ever known. Fred, fours years my junior, was a bit of an embarrassment to me at this juncture. He became deeply interested in insects and all sorts of creepy-crawly things! I was, at times, mortified when my friends would see Fred running around with his butterfly net and specimen bottle! To this day, Fred, at age sixty-eight, is thoroughly immersed in the study of insects. He volunteers at the local high school to teach his love of insects to the science students. I am proud of him now! It is quite a distinction to be the brother of a leading entomologist!

All good things must come to an end. In 1952, once again the Lord and the bishop sent us packing, this time to Roanoke, Virginia, to Greene Memorial Methodist Church. Thus ended one of the happiest periods of my life.

Chapter 3 (Ann)

(1966 – 1968)

It was nice to be in Alabama: good food, nice people and warm weather. Amerigo Marino, the conductor of the orchestra, was – if I remember rightly – a former pupil of Leonard Bernstein, and he was wonderful. He had conducted the Berlin Orchestra when he was only twelve! The lady who played principal flute and I (second chair) worked well together. The university was convenient and all I needed to do to complete my degree was take an academic class and a few musical subjects to build up enough credits to allow me to graduate from that institution. I learned to drive and bought a little car. Life was good.

There is just one black mark against my early days in Birmingham and that really had more to do with my time in Richmond, after the road accident. While I was living with my parents I was lonely. My former high school friends had all dispersed and Mother and Dad worked long hours. My only company was the television. The soap stars were the only people I saw for a year and a half, and they became very real to me – so real that I would have to stop myself from telling my parents what had happened to so-and-so that day. And, of course, my head had been badly hurt when I was run over, damaged to the degree that it was several days before the doctors decided I would not be retarded. Actually, I can remember the 'day of reckoning' quite well. I was asked if I knew where I was, and I looked at all the traction over my head and I thought I was in prison. However, what I said was, "In a hospital," and then I wondered why I knew that (I didn't remember that I had been told this repeatedly for several days). Then I was asked if I knew which hospital, and I was again surprised to hear myself answering, "Lakeside." I had been told that on a regular basis, too. But I had a long process of re-learning little facts and figures. I drove my mother mad by constantly asking things like, "What kind of tree is that? Isn't that a pretty flower! What is it called?" Well, I think she was pleased that I had the use of my mind, no matter how irritating that made me.

One evening in Birmingham I lapsed back into my fantasy life. I thought I was watching someone in a soap opera take too many pills; I didn't realize I was doing it myself. Some friends stopped by, saw what was happening and took me to the hospital for a stomach pump. It turned out that I was not in any real danger – I was high on aspirin and had a therapeutic dosage of bromides. And then, two large and imposing uniformed policemen came to tell me that it is illegal to commit suicide. I may have been in a strange world of my own, but that didn't stop me from recognizing the absurdity of being arrested for killing myself. I suppose they could put my ashes behind bars!

This whole experience put the fear of God into me and I threw away any and every kind of pill I had, and I never again allowed myself to relapse into my fantasy world. And it was many years before I watched another soap opera. Not until 'Dallas' arrived, in fact.

The following spring, I was offered the first flute position in an after-season touring orchestra. We travelled thousands of miles, frequently playing two concerts a day. Unfortunately, the conductor was not a Bernstein protégé and the orchestra was not the New York Philharmonic! But it was an interesting experience nonetheless. And I met a young man, a trumpeter, who cared enough to follow me to Alabama.

Do you think it's possible to sense the future? The academic subject I chose to study at the university was Abnormal Psychology. My beautiful boyfriend went crazy.

They happened slowly, the changes in Jay's moods and way of thinking, and at first I, simple soul that I am, made light of the mood swings. For instance, some teenage boys had an old jeep which they had painted psychedelic colours. Jay fixated on this, but I laughed it off. "They're just boys with more money than brains," I said, unoriginally.

But when Jay took a short plane journey and was flying over the clouds, he realized he could communicate with his father. His natural father and God his father seemed to be confused. When I heard this, I couldn't hide from the fact that he was not well. Then one evening after an orchestra concert, we were driving along in my car, Jay's housemate Pete and girlfriend in the back seat, when Jay became vehement about his need to talk to the FBI. He jumped out of the car and ran off. We finally located him in the Sheriff's office demanding protection. I had a quiet word with the officer and he agreed to let Jay stay in the lock-up overnight, but he couldn't hold him against his will; he would, he said, telephone me when Jay released himself.

So the two friends with me went off to contact Jay's mother and I went home to try to locate Jay's father. His parents were divorced, and Jay's father had remarried. The telephone operator was wonderful. The only information I had to give her was that he had the same name as his son and that he owned an electrical shop in Tampa, Florida. The operator located him.

How do you tell a man his son is mentally ill? I introduced myself as Jay's girlfriend, and his voice was immediately warm and welcoming. I blurted out that his son was ill and I didn't know what to do. He said he would arrive in Birmingham the next day. The police rang me in the morning to tell me Jay had left the station but they had no idea where he had gone. Pete stayed at home in case Jay showed up there, and I stayed in my flat in case he returned to me. Jay finally arrived at my place shortly before his father.

Jay's father took him to his home in Tampa for a week, had a prayer said for him and then sent him back to Birmingham. His mother sent him a book on Christian Science. Jay treasured the book and kept saying, "This is the truth! This is the truth!" He showed me a passage which said that doctors can't be trusted because sometimes they say drugs are good for you, but they also say drugs are bad for you. Now, I have a dilemma here, because I believe strongly in the power of the mind and I can understand the allure of Christian Science; but Jay's mind was sick. That book his mother sent pretty much destroyed any chance I might have had of getting him to a doctor. That's unfair of me; there was no way Jay would see a shrink, book or no book.

Although Jay was largely inarticulate the few times he tried to share his worries with me, I managed to piece his fears together. In a nutshell, he believed that his father, God, had warned him of a plot by the communists to take over the world. He also heard voices discussing their intentions. At the forefront of the invasion were the boys with the jeep. The plan was to get people high on marijuana and then hypnotize them into becoming communists. It sounds stupid, but I can assure you it was very frightening.

I talked to my psychology professor about what help I could get for Jay, but there wasn't really anything I could do unless I married him and then had him committed – which would be a long and messy business. Although I don't think Jay would have hurt me, he did once – at this point I had just begun to realize that he no longer trusted me – turn around suddenly while holding a butcher knife. It was one of those electrically charged moments when two people share the same thought. He suggested I leave, and I did. Fast. The orchestra season was over and my mother came down from Richmond and helped me move out of my flat. I finished the last term of university living in the dormitory.

I've sometimes wondered if I was attracted to Jay because, having been through the episode with the pills, I could relate so closely to his schizophrenia.

Those particular years, the mid-sixties, were very important in the history of America. Civil Rights activists were demonstrating around the country. My parents, though they never rammed their beliefs down anyone's throat, were firm believers in the equality of race and gender. Once, when they were running an insurance agency, they were invited by an African-American client (actually, the term 'African American' had not been invented at this time; he would have been called 'black') to attend a service in his church. Mother confessed to feeling some trepidation but they accepted the offer. They were welcomed warmly by the Pastor, who introduced them as friends of some members of the congregation. They had a wonderful time! And yet I don't remember my parents ever going back to that church. Nor do I remember the invitation being reciprocated.

When I was seven or eight, I was riding in a bus in Richmond with my mother. The back of the bus was crowded, but there were seats available at the front; yet one black woman was standing. "Mommy," I said loudly, "why is that lady standing?" Even I, at that tender age, felt the tension! We got off at the next stop. In the fifties and early sixties, black people sat only at the back of a bus.

And while I was living in Alabama, I made friends with two black girls. That is, we wanted to be friends, but it wasn't possible. They drove me to my flat one afternoon, and they made me sit in the back seat by myself. For my safety, it was to show that I didn't socialize with coloured people. For their safety, it showed they didn't associate with white people. They refused to come in for coffee, saying my neighbours would likely 'string me up' if I entertained them in my home. It was very sad.

When Martin Luther King was shot (1968), the only safe way to drive was to keep your headlights on as a sign of respect. And now we have had a woman and a coloured man battling it out for the Democratic nomination! Things have certainly changed.

And speaking of change, that's exactly what was needed in my life after the worries and heartache of the whole business with Jay; I had originally thought we would eventually marry and instead I found myself running away from him. With the remainder of the insurance money, I went to London to study at the Royal Academy of Music.

Chapter 4 (Bob)

(1953 – 1962)

My high school career was a total concentration of music, not only playing the trumpet in the high school band but also, more importantly, in the dance bands in and around Danville. I was very fortunate to be in a position to earn what was in that day big money. I did find time for Suzie. Ah, sweet memories! We went 'steady' for three years. Her parents were members of my father's church, and for this reason I was admonished to conduct myself 'in a gentlemanly manner'. Suzie was a very petite and well-endowed young lass. Some thirty or so years later, I was in Danville to play at a church and Susie was in the audience. I uttered a silent prayer of thanksgiving when she and I met. The darling girl's petite physique had blossomed into one of gargantuan proportions!

My best friend, Bob Hill, graduated a year earlier than I. He entered R.P.I. (Richmond Professional Institute) as a clarinet and oboe major. Bob and I were very close throughout his life and I officiated at his funeral in 1997 in Savannah, Georgia.

Bob was forced to retire on disability at age forty-two, shortly after he and his family moved to Savannah. I don't recall the medical reason for his disability, but alcohol was to become his downfall and the cause of his untimely death. Bob's last years were spent listening to classical music, helping with the Savannah Youth Symphony, volunteering on the local National Public Radio Station as an announcer, reporter and disc jockey from time to time, and immersing himself in his favourite beverages. Bob's wife, Kitty, is a lovely woman, a fine singer, and if there were an award for 'Wife of the Century', I would nominate her for the honour.

It was in the summer of 1953 that my family moved to Roanoke. My musical life was severely hampered. I auditioned for the Roanoke Symphony and was given the second trumpet chair. My first encounter with classical music was a godsend – an encounter that was to shape my life from then on. I studied voice with the Minister of Music at the church. She was a former pupil of John Finley Williamson, founder and president of the Westminster Choir College, a prestigious music conservatory for church musicians. These lessons would prove to be beneficial years in the future.

Upon my father's insistence, I enrolled at Randolph-Macon College in Ashland, Virginia. I was able to land a trumpet gig each week playing at the Wigwam on Fridays and the Starlight Club on Saturdays. Each Tuesday evening, I went to Richmond to play in the orchestra at R.P.I. The conductor of the orchestra was a gentleman I grew to love and admire. His name was Milton Cherry.

I mustered all the courage my nineteen years would allow and sat my father down and simply told him I was leaving Randolph Macon College (a breeding place for new Methodist Ministers). I told him, with all the respect I could muster, that either he could assist me in attending R.P.I. where I would major in Music Education (knowing full well that I would pursue a degree in performance), or else I was prepared to join the US Navy. Thank God he agreed to back my musical studies, else I would have spent my life bobbing up and down in an ocean somewhere as a seasick member of a Navy band!

In January 1954, I entered R.P.I. as a trumpet major. The teacher of brass instruments was a German, H.C.E. Schmidt, who happened to be eighty-five years old. He had a definite dislike for contemporary music. He also had a terrible hatred for jazz, and when he found out I was playing in dance bands to help fund my very existence, he set out to radically change my embouchure (mouthpiece placement). This tactic resulted in returning me to grade four as a trumpet player and ending my livelihood. What had been my most enjoyable activity immediately became my most dreaded one – playing the trumpet. This method on the dear old octogenarian's part caused me to determine to change my major at the beginning of my sophomore year. This served a dual purpose: it would eliminate Herr Schmidt from my life as well as give me a 10 – 90 % chance of reclaiming a life of music. All this at the tender age of twenty!

The Faculty of the School of Music gave their guarded consent for me to change my major instrument from trumpet to clarinet. In my junior year, I would be required to give a joint recital with another instrumentalist. In my senior year, I would have to give a full recital from the major repertoire of the clarinet. I agreed, and promised the faculty I would meet the requirements and more. Herr Schmidt sat there and glared at me. He knew what he had done! To help me on my accelerated journey, I travelled to Washington, DC every other week to study with Wallace Kramer of the US Army Band at Fort Meyers. He was an extraordinary player. More importantly, he was one of the finest clarinet teachers ever to come my way. The nine months I studied clarinet with Kramer was the icing on the cake which, combined with untold hours of practice, cemented my sophomoric foolishness into what was to become a most successful endeavour.

I would like to come up to the twenty-first century for just a moment to make an observation. The human body is not designed to do one physical task repeatedly, over and over, day in and day out. I firmly believe this period of concentration and accelerated practising on the clarinet (usually six hours or more a day) is the major cause, some fifty years later, of the emergence of incapacitating arthritis in both of my hands. In later years, I would encourage my students to adopt the mindset – 'Work Smart, Not Hard.'

The beginning of my junior year witnessed a stroke of phenomenal good fortune. Bennett Reimer was employed by the school as the teacher of woodwinds.

(I think it was during my junior year that Mr Cherry brought his daughter, Ann, to the music school. I remember seeing this little girl, slight of build with dark hair. I secretly wished she had been about five years older! I have not seen her since this time. We were reacquainted over the internet in 2005).

Reimer was fresh out of graduate school at the University of Illinois. I was now twenty years old. My new teacher was every bit of twenty-three! With Reimer's guidance and support, that year I got to perform Bartók's *Contrasts* for clarinet, violin and piano, a wonderful work. Bartók, himself a violinist, recorded this work in 1940 with Joseph Szigeti and Benny Goodman. I performed it with my mentor and musical god, Milton Cherry of the school faculty. Cherry was a little younger than my father by only a few years. He became, if only in my mind, a father figure during these conservatory years.

My junior year was the best of my undergraduate career. Of particular importance was that, feeling the long hours of clarinet practice needed to be balanced with a recreational activity, I chose to learn the flute. It was simply a fun activity; I took no lessons. I was not trying to impress anyone, not meeting deadlines, not practising unless I felt like it. In other words, I did everything most teachers frown upon. I *enjoyed* playing the flute poorly!

I was fortunate enough to rent a room in a run down antebellum home within easy walking distance of the music building. The year culminated in the Junior Recital. My Junior Recital was an ambitious one for someone who was only in the second year of playing clarinet. The programme consisted of the Brahms *E Flat Sonata*, Stravinsky's *Three Pieces* for Solo Clarinet and the wonderful *Trio* by Ernst Krenek for clarinet, violin and piano, all extremely difficult works. Again, Milton Cherry graced the recital with his marvellous violin as he played the violin part of this trio.

The next year, 1956-57, was spent with the knowledge that if I was to graduate in June of 1957, I had to start taking my academic work seriously! The remainder of my time was spent between the clarinet and Nancy. Nancy was a gifted contralto singer. She was very small, maybe five-feet tall, and weighed no more than 105 pounds. She had the biggest, most powerful contralto voice I ever heard. She sang the Brahms *Alto Rhapsody* on her recital and it was amazing. Nancy was a few years older than I, separated from her husband who was in Cincinnati, Ohio. At this time, separation and divorce were frowned upon. To date a married woman, even if she were separated from her husband was, to the genteel social graces of Virginia, unacceptable. Needless to say, my dear parents were pretty upset with me. Neither Nancy nor I entertained any idea of marriage or commitment. Music was first and foremost in our minds and hearts. I heard some years later that Nancy had committed suicide. She developed polyps on her vocal chords, and the surgeon, during an operation to remove them, slipped and his scalpel severed her vocal chords. It broke her heart. I was devastated when I learned this.

In my senior year, I became determined to go to Vienna and study with Leopold Vlach. He was, at that time, the clarinettist whom I considered next to the Almighty in the scheme of things. As cruel fate would have it, Vlach died before I could study with him. Since time was of the essence (I didn't want to be drafted!), I selected Northwestern University as the place to do my graduate work. I made the decision after visiting the Peabody Conservatory of Music in Baltimore, Maryland. I was not at all impressed!

I was to be the first graduate student in Northwestern's history to enter as a clarinet graduate student in performance. All other clarinettists matriculated previously as Music Education majors with a concentration in clarinet. The truth of the matter was, I selected this school to study with their rather famous clarinet teacher, whose name I cannot now remember! The years are not a kind custodian of one's memory! Lo and behold, when I arrived on the campus in Evanston, Illinois, the clarinet teacher had taken a sabbatical leave to study and play in Vienna. My teacher at Northwestern now was to be Jerome (Jerry) Stowell, the E-flat clarinettist with the Chicago Symphony Orchestra under Fritz Reiner. He was a pleasant kind of chap who never made any demands on his students. And he never once brought his clarinet to a lesson. It would have been nice to have played a duet or two with my exalted professor. He did give me an 'A' for the year and also for my recital at the conclusion of the year.

With no clear motive, other than the sheer delight of fiddling with the flute, I took lessons from the head of the flute department at Northwestern, Emil Eck. He was a fine, fine flutist and a marvellous teacher. He was also endowed with a remarkable amount of patience. I suspect, knowing that I was studying flute just 'for the fun of it', he and I approached lessons as a break from the rigours of the fast-paced life at the university. I became friends with John Meacham, a wonderful young flutist. John was a bit older than I, and he had served in the army as the principal flutist with the Army Band at West Point. He helped me immensely by playing duets from time to time, and the year drew to a close much more quickly than I ever dreamed it would. My post-graduate recital was given in Lutkin Hall in May of 1958. I played the Mozart *Clarinet Quintet.* In addition to the Mozart, I did Weber's *Grand Duo Concertante* and the Stravinsky *Three Pieces.*

My graduate recital went very well, and I deserved the 'A' I had been given! The day after the recital, I did something that was to prove to be prophetic: I sold my LeBlanc clarinets. To this day, fifty years later, I have never regretted this. At the time it did not seem very significant to me. Little did I realize how powerful that act would prove to be. It was like being let out of jail! By the way, I did *not* sell my Gemeinhardt flute.

Not having the foggiest understanding of what was happening, I was well on my way to a career as a flutist! Little did I suspect what would take place during the next fifty years! I met Ann Hall at R.P.I. She was to become my bride in 1958. I discovered she and I lived fairly close to each other. We dated during the summer of my senior year. By the time I left for graduate school, we were in love and were planning to get married after I finished my graduate work.

Knowing that there were precious few ways to escape military service, I set out to do it the best I could. I signed a contract to teach band in Tappahannock, Virginia, on a Thursday. I received that dreaded letter from Uncle Sam on Saturday. The letter commenced, 'Your friends and neighbours...' I would be drafted since the letter was mailed before I signed the teaching contract. Teachers were deferred and I wasn't a teacher. Students were deferred and I was not a student. Fathers were deferred and I wasn't a father! I married Ann on June 28, 1958. A day or so after the blessed nuptials, Congress did away with the marriage deferment! In case you think I married to keep my deferment from military service, that is not at all true. But it would have been nice had it turned out so.

I was certain the good Lord wanted me in uniform. I reported for military service on September 15, 1958. Ann was a loving wife who sacrificed much in those days. We were happy for many years and raised two wonderful children. I have to say, she put up with more than any human being should have to put up with! I arrived at Fort Jackson, South Carolina, September 15, 1958, wondering if I would ever play again! All in all, it was probably good for a young man who had spent most of his adult life in a practice room. I learned to fire the various military weapons, to fear commissioned officers, and to get along with men from all walks of life. I realized that music, though my passion, was not always important to others. Upon completion of Basic Training, I was assigned to the Band Training Unit at Fort Jackson. It was my job to teach bandsmen sent there from all over the Third Army Command in an accelerated four weeks Basic Army Bandsman Course.

At Christmas time, I had a few weeks of leave and went to Virginia to visit my new bride. We decided, on the spur of the moment, that she would accompany me to Fort Jackson. We arrived after the long drive in the 1953 Ford. Only one flat tyre marred the trip. We rented a small, dilapidated apartment and set up housekeeping. We were young and happy. The band at Fort Jackson owned a Haynes flute. I checked it out and found that my dear Gemeinhardt flute was not as fine an instrument as I had believed. I had never held a piccolo in my hand, and hope never to do so again. My Army Bandsman career was spent discovering that the piccolo should have been nicknamed the *Prince of Misery*. In the end, I did learn to play the damnable piccolo. But only because I had no choice!

In September 1959, I received orders to go to Fulda, Germany, to play flute in a twenty-eight piece band. I looked Fulda up on a map and found it was located on the German-Russian border. One who had been there told me you could look out of the barracks window and see the Russian soldiers looking back at you. After so short a time living with my new wife, she took me to Fort Dix, New Jersey, and waved goodbye as the USS Buckner, a WW2 troop ship, pulled away from the dock on the way to Bremen. One of life's most important and unusual quirks of fate occurred to me in the middle of the Atlantic Ocean aboard the rusty, creaky, old USS Buckner. The ship had a very loud public address system. One day as I was throwing up over the rail (I stayed sea sick for the entire seven day trip), an announcement came over the public address system, "Private Hawkins, report to the Bridge." After exchanging salutes, the skipper showed me a revised set of US Army Orders with my name and serial number on it. The orders had been cut because someone interceded on my behalf. I have no idea who it was, but I owe that person a debt of gratitude!

Instead of heading for the band in Fulda, I was now assigned to the Seventh Army Symphony Orchestra in Stuttgart, Germany! I had packed my little silver-plated Gemeinhardt flute in my duffle bag. How much I wanted to take it out and practise! I knew if I did, I would either be thrown in the brig or buried at sea. Upon arrival in Stuttgart, I was given a few weeks to practise the flute and live a normal life. I found the Symphony to be truly one of the best orchestras I had ever heard. The young members were recent Eastman, Julliard, Curtis and Manhattan School of Music graduates, as well as a smattering of other top music schools. There was an over-supply of flutists and I was sent to the Seventh Army Band located in the next building. The idea was when they needed me, I would come back to the orchestra.

I spent the next two years as the principal flutist with the band. As far as military bands go, this was a rather good musical aggregation. The normal daily routine was as follows: concert band rehearsal from 8am 'til eleven o'clock; after lunch we would have a rehearsal of the show band; and marching band before dinner. I was made the director of the Chorus. Made up of the men in the band, we occasionally sang in concerts. I enjoyed this new experience and it was to stand me in good stead in later life. One of the missions the Army had chosen for us was to play all over Germany for both beer and wine fests! Basically, it went like this: the band would travel in three or four buses to the beer fest. Inside a gigantic tent lined with tables and raucous inebriated Germans, we would play overtures, show tunes, polkas and marches. The musicians were able to consume huge amounts of good German beer. In May of 1960, Ann joined me in Germany. Immediately she became pregnant, and for the next nine months I was on the road constantly with the band while she stayed in our apartment in downtown Stuttgart. The band spent most of this time touring Europe. The most amazing concert tour was to Lucerne, Switzerland. International treaties forbade any military organization from wearing military uniforms in Switzerland. The band gave concerts nightly, alternating with the Big Jazz Band. This was one of the most enjoyable tours I had during my two-year stay in the

Seventh Army Band: playing jazz in civilian clothes for two weeks in Switzerland! It didn't get much better than that!

In March of 1961, Ann and I became the parents of Lillian, our first-born, and in May of 1961, Ann and the baby left for the United States. To finance their plane fare on Air France, I sold my Haynes flute for $200. I think I neglected to mention that I had purchased a second-hand Haynes flute while in Germany. The tickets were $160! I still had my old Gemeinhardt. I was reminded of the biblical text, 'We came into the world with nothing, and will leave it with nothing.' After they left Germany, I killed time until it was time for me to return home on – you guessed it – the venerable USS Buckner! I arrived at the Brooklyn Army Terminal after a lovely cruise from Germany in July 1962. After a short leave and time to reacquaint myself with American life, we (Ann, Lillian and I) were stationed in Brooklyn, New York, for the remainder of my enlistment. On April 2, 1962 I was honourably discharged from the United States Army.

Chapter 5 (Ann)

(1968 – 1978)

The Royal Academy of Music audition consisted of playing a piece for the Principal only; in fact, he accompanied me. I played the little Chopin Variations and the Principal (I can't remember his name) was so drunk he couldn't keep up. I had to do a little sight-reading and then I was in. For the first time in my life, I found myself with a flute teacher – Derek Honner – who actually tried to work on my strange double-jointed fingers. Derek was a wonderful teacher, retired some time ago. I fell deeply in love with London, a fabulous city with five major orchestras, opera, chamber music, and all of it reachable by public transport. I went to concerts five or six evenings a week for six months before I even considered doing something else. I learned more in those six months of listening than I did from any teacher – my parents complained that my letters were nothing but concert reviews! You know, I never understood it when my pupils didn't go to concerts. It's the best way to learn! Anyway, where was I? Dietrich Fischer-Dieskau was giving a baritone voice and piano recital and I had bought a ticket for it. I nearly didn't go – a voice recital in a large orchestral hall and my seat at the very back? It was bound to be boring. But it still stands out in my mind as the best concert I have ever heard in the whole of my life. The man had such presence that when he walked onto the stage, and before he opened his mouth, you were down on the platform with him. It was stunning!

I lived in a music club where I met people giving debut recitals, and I felt that I was as good as some of them (that damned ego of mine!). So I set up my debut with financial help from the Music and Drama Club of Cleveland, Ohio. Mother and Dad were trying to get me to return home because my year was over (my course had finished in July) and I was now spending their money and not mine, so I sold my piccolo to pay the rent. The debut went well – 14 January, 1970. *The Daily Telegraph* gave me a bang-up review and two years later, when I once again moved to London – after Italy – they supported me through my career by coming to my recitals and giving me good reviews.

These were the days of the miniskirt, and that's what I was wearing on the leaflets for my debut. A freelance cameraman saw the handouts and contacted me, saying he wanted to take a photo which he could sell to a newspaper. If he succeeded, I would get some free publicity for my debut. Naturally, I agreed. What I didn't realize was that he would sell it as a 'Page 3' story! (Page 3 is for pictures of voluptuous women; the photographer had to do some touching up in my case!). But they say no news is all bad, and I recovered from my huff the next day when the BBC, having seen the newspaper item, asked me to play and be interviewed on their overseas programme.

Altogether I went to Severino Gazzelloni's course in Siena for three summers. There didn't seem to be much sense in returning to Richmond between summers, so I enrolled in the Conservatory St Cecilia in Rome.

Gazzelloni's English was as bad as my Italian, and somehow he got it into his head that he should speak to me in French. My Italian was better than my French! I soon realized that the way to learn from Severo was to ask him to demonstrate and then copy. I'll say this much for that approach – it teaches you to analyse.

Gazzelloni and I had a love/hate relationship. When I made him unhappy, he would ignore me in his class (lessons were always in a group). When he made me angry, I wouldn't go to his class.

While I was in Rome I was invited to become part of a new music ensemble. It was an excellent chamber group, and eye-opening for me who had believed, until then, that most *avant-garde* music was junk. This decided me to stay a little longer in Rome. (And I spent the next ten years of my life specializing in this strange and wonderful music.) The ensemble, called the Forum Players, toured throughout southern Europe, appeared on Greek television, radio in several countries, music festivals in Spain, and we even went to Tunisia. One of the things I regularly performed was Davidovsky's *Synchronisms* for flute and pre-recorded electronic sounds. Somewhere in Turkey – maybe Ankara – the person operating the tape was in a sealed control room and couldn't hear that he had threaded the tape badly. It wobbled all over the place and I had to stay with it! I was asked to play *Synchronisms* for Greek educational TV, and this time *I* was the one who couldn't hear the tape! Fortunately, I had played it so often that I managed to get the speeds okay and it worked.

I also played Berio's *Sequenza,* the first piece that called for a double-tone on the flute. This had to be done by relaxing the lip enough to play both the main note and the harmonic at the same time – you know, one of those things one spends years learning *not* to do. I can vouch for the fact that it's a difficult technique to manage if you're nervous!

One tour was very nearly too exciting. We were waiting at the airport in Istanbul for our plane to arrive but it never came. It turned out that the plane was hijacked in Ankara –

the stop just before ours – by Turkish leftist militants and taken to Sofia (this was in May 1972). As I remember, no one was hurt.

I had quite a fright in Rome when I was picked up by the police for armed robbery. I was standing in the queue in the American Express building in Rome, waiting my turn to cash a cheque. There was a black man behind me, although I didn't realize it until I was finishing my transaction and he asked me, "Are you through?" I said yes, and left.

I met some friends for lunch that day in Trastevere, a tourist area of Rome, and bought a Perry Mason novel in Italian from a book stall – well, perhaps not the highbrow taste I should have had, but good for learning a little basic Italian without the idioms! When I returned to my flat that afternoon, the concierge told me the police wanted to see me. Sure enough, they arrived immediately. They told me I'd made a mistake in my student visa stuff and they said they would take me to the station to sort it out. It seemed excessive, but I accepted it and went with them.

When I arrived at the station, it became obvious they didn't want to talk to me about visas! They questioned me about my movements that day and how could I say I didn't know the man behind me at the Am Ex building when I was seen talking to him? They confiscated my Perry Mason book for quite a while; I assume they were looking for something inside the book, maybe a message. They may even have checked with the stall where I purchased it – they kept it for long enough. After a couple of hours, the police brought in one of the people I had met up with for lunch (checking my alibi, I suppose). At one point they left my friend, Jim, and me alone together, with a policeman on guard who apparently spoke no English. Jim and I just made small talk until another policeman popped in, holding a man's T-shirt, and asked me if I recognized it. I think I was bordering on hysteria at this point as the realization that I was in big trouble sank in, and I burst out laughing at the idea that suspects were walking around the streets without shirts. Suddenly, the Policeman-Who-Spoke-No-English said sharply to me:

"Why are you laughing?"

He had to leave for blowing his cover!

Jim and I were put into the back of a police car and taken to another police station. There are different kinds of police in Italy, but I no longer remember the distinction. We were questioned for three more hours and then released.

In Italy in those days there was a lot of prejudice against blacks, and a white woman who had any kind of relationship with a black man was lower than the lowest.

I rang my parents and told them what was going on because in Italy, the police could lock you up for a year without pressing charges or telling anyone where you are. I wanted them to know about this business in case I disappeared.

The next day I realized the same person seemed always to be where I was. The police must have thought I was blind or stupid to pick such incompetent cops to follow me. I was tailed for three days, but some of it was fun. My little crowd of friends went to a concert given by the Fires of London, an excellent English *avant-garde* ensemble. We were sitting in the balcony and, as is the case so often with concerts of modern music, the hall was half empty. An usher came to tell those of us in the cheap balcony seats that we could move downstairs if we wished. Everybody in the balcony got up and moved downstairs, except my little group – and one man on his own. At the end of the concert, this man followed us backstage and was clearly embarrassed at having to thank the performers (I would hazard a guess that he had never been to a concert before in his life!). He overheard us arranging to meet the members of the Fires in the local bar, and then he left – to be in the bar when we arrived.

The police removed my tail after that event. But I kept running into the black man whose shirt I was asked to identify. He told me the police picked him up three times. He also told me the outcome of this robbery: it was staged by one of the Italian cashiers, who wrote a note saying something like, 'I have a gun. Put money in this bag', and then claimed the black man had written it. I was thought to be in cahoots with the black man because he had talked to me at the American Express office.

While I was living it up – or otherwise – in Rome, my parents were planning their retirement. They, quite rightly, determined that I should settle down and start earning a proper income. Mother and Daddy wanted to move to England where their American pensions would stretch further. They also wanted to live near one of their children and that meant something had to be done about me – I would have to get settled there first. Mother wrote letters in my name to various schools until she found one that knew how to get me a work permit. The English government said I could not work in London where I would be taking a job away from an Englishman, but Trinity College of Music gave me an interview anyway and said to let them know if I got around the work permit problem. Westonbirt School for Girls, in Gloucester, got the permit for me, gave me a position teaching flute and also found some more teaching for me in the area. I didn't go to England to live in Gloucestershire, so I commuted from London. Never rely on British Rail to get you to work on time!

I had no experience in teaching, but I did have enough sense not to admit it! I turned out to be quite good with the students, but I found Westonbirt quite difficult to settle into because it was a boarding school. Many of the students were homesick, but there was one American girl who touched my heart; she was so lonely. She looked forward to our lessons because I was like a breath of American air. I don't think the Head of Music liked me much; I can only think that perhaps she hadn't wanted my appointment. Trying to be nice, I suggested that we prepare a short concert with the singing teacher. We gave it up for being too difficult to arrange rehearsal times, but really I think all three of us realized it wouldn't work. Whenever the soprano sang, I had to control the most awful urge to indulge in hysterical laughter. She had plenty of ability, but not much knowledge of differing styles. Yes, I admit it, and shamelessly: I am a musical snob.

I spent Thursday nights in a charming teachers' cottage on the school grounds. Here was another tricky situation: I gave up eating dinner with the rest of the staff because I ate slowly and these English women ate quickly. Somehow they managed to pile food two inches high with the fork upside down. And they thought *my* manners were odd! I took extra sandwiches for my two days of peripatetic teaching in Gloucester, and twice used the cottage's kitchen to make a cup of tea in the morning. Then I gave that up too. Imagine four elderly spinsters living together for years, then along comes someone new, upsetting the routine…

"Elvira, the cooker's hot! Did you leave it on all night?"

"Who's been using *my* water?"

"Myrtle, have the teabags been moved?"

I carried a bottle of coke from then on!

On Friday mornings I visited a little town called Dursley. This must have been the best teaching job in the world! The Head of Music – I've forgotten his name – loved music and loved students, and they all adored him. My Dursley students all got high marks on their exams and practised because they wanted to, not because they were told to. I was 'flavour of the month' and had a waiting list of students who wanted to study with me. The female pupils even copied my hairstyle.

Moving to England meant settling down. Settling down meant getting married. I met a young man in London who charmed me with his Cockney accent and soon we were living together. My parents announced their date for moving to England, and I didn't want them to know I was 'living in sin', so Charlie and I tied the knot (it was always our intention to marry anyway). I am the only person I know whose husband made a pass at another woman on their honeymoon. I should have had the marriage annulled, but I had this stupid American belief that if you want a thing bad enough, you can make it happen. I wanted this marriage to work.

At this time I was getting up at 5am on a Thursday morning in order to catch the first train to Gloucestershire, spending the night there, teaching all day for those two days and returning late Friday night; and then getting up early Saturday morning to go to Winchester to teach junior exhibitioners, finally returning home Saturday evening. I could not afford to leave this work, financially or morally. Morally, because lots of people marry in order to stay in the country, but I had a valid work permit and I intended to honour it. Financially, because it seems my husband couldn't keep a job. I did contact Trinity College of Music and they offered me a position, so I added that to my teaching. Three months later, the London College of Music offered me some teaching, so I took that on as well. My starting salary at Trinity was £2.70 an hour; the LCM proudly said they could offer me more and gave me £2.90 per hour. Neither sum was a living wage.

I was still trying to practise every day. Whenever I gave a concert I got virtually no support from Charlie, who seemed to think performing on stage was the same as picking up a guitar at a party and making up silly songs.

Over the weeks things worsened. It seemed that every time I went to Gloucestershire something awful happened. Charlie lost his job (that was when I learned he had a criminal record, albeit not for something too serious). He lost the next job too, and this turned into a regular thing. Eventually he found a job, driving for a chauffeuring firm, which he managed to keep. But the regular Friday night disasters still kept happening. One time I learned that he had passed out at work and had been taken to hospital. Another time he told me he had been contacted by a woman with whom he'd had an affair as a teenager, and this woman informed him she had a daughter of which he was the father. I was devastated, but I said to Charlie, if he wanted a divorce so he could marry this other woman, I would let him go. I also suggested he apply for visiting rights. Is it any wonder that the walk home from the tube station each Friday got harder and harder? Sometimes my legs would barely move. For thirteen weeks in a row there was some kind of disaster, and then it dawned on me: none of it was true.

His excuse was, he didn't like my going away overnight. Maybe not, but he apparently found company while I was away. I know because one evening, around midnight, the doorbell rang and a woman introduced herself to me as someone who had been sleeping with my husband. She may have been, but she seemed awfully butch, and when she was leaving she said to me, "You're really very pretty," and leaned over to kiss me. If I hadn't turned my head, her kiss would have landed on my mouth!

I had a little motorcycle at this time to save on tube fares into London, and she let the air out of the tyres that night. Bitch!

I gave the marriage one more shot. I borrowed enough money from my parents to allow us to move into a little house rather than staying in a rented flat. I thought maybe pride of ownership would make Charlie feel good. In fact, it didn't make any difference at all. One day we affably shared a tube journey into London, I to my teaching, Charlie to stay at a friend's flat near to his latest *inamorata*. The marriage was finally finished.

Yecch, what a fiasco the whole thing was!

Charlie and I married in 1974 and divorced in 1978. Mother and Dad arrived in England in 1975. They did the only thing they could – they kept out of my personal problems. After we broke up, Daddy referred to Charlie as a pathological liar. Which he was. I've left out the bits where he made passes at my female friends; and I was afraid to leave him alone with my private female pupils. On top of that, he showed up one evening at Trinity College of Music drunk. It wasn't nice.

The last Christmas Charlie and I spent together we went to a party given by a friend of his. I don't remember his name. It was obvious something was up and I was careful not to drink too much. Charlie and his friend and the friend's wife were whispering together and all were trying to get me to consume a large quantity of alcohol. Have you ever spent several hours at a party carrying the same half empty glass of wine and assuring everyone that the glass had just been topped up? It's not easy. But while I was sober, they were not. I overheard Charlie saying to our host, "She's like a faithful dog; you have to go slow." It's bad enough to realize that your husband is conspiring to get you so drunk that you agree to a wife swapping. It's unforgivable that he calls you a faithful dog! The outcome was, I threw a tantrum and they tried to deny it until I quoted their comments back to them.

In hindsight I can see that we both made mistakes. I was imposing my ideals and goals on Charlie. But that's no excuse for his showing up at my workplace drunk, or making passes at my friends. My marriage to Charlie left me with such a disgust of men that it was a whole year before I recovered enough to socialize. My confidence was zero. What kind of woman was I if my husband, who at one time had professed to love me, felt I deserved no loyalty? Then one day I decided to pick up the first man I met, just to prove I could do it. Well, it was ridiculously easy. I went to the motorcycle shop I dealt with and chatted up the owner. He was engaged to be married, but I didn't care. Let the woman have some of my kind of pain, I thought. And who knows? Maybe if the shop owner had kept his mouth shut our so-called affair might have amounted to something. But he made the mistake of wanting to talk, and I realized he was a klutz.

Chapter 6 (Bob)

(1962 – 1976)

No sooner had Ann, Lillian and I returned home to Richmond, Virginia, in April of 1962, than the stark realization sank in that I had a wife and an infant who were dependent on me for life's necessities. Other than school teaching and church choir work, there was little available for a classically trained musician to do to earn a living.

As luck would have it, the economy was in good shape in 1962. One Sunday morning I scanned the classified section of the *Richmond Times Dispatch* and found two job possibilities: one in banking and the other in retailing. Kierkegaard's 'leap of faith' for me resembled more a 'leap of reality'. The following day I put on my only suit and caught a city bus for 6th and Broad Street, the main branch of Thalhimers, the growing department store giant in the early 1960s. I was ushered into the Divisional Merchandise Manager's office and asked if I had graduated from college, as this was a requirement for applicants to the Junior Executive Training Program. I responded in the affirmative. My newly-found career involved extremely long hours as well as learning the Fine Jewellery business. I worked as the Assistant Buyer for the Fine Jewellery and Silver Departments for a relatively short time – about fourteen months. An unexpected turn of events was in my favour. My boss, George Brothers, the Jewellery and Silver Buyer, left the store for a more lucrative job at Davidson's Department

Store in Atlanta, Georgia. I was asked to manage things until his replacement could be hired. After approximately two months, I was offered the position, and I readily accepted it. At age twenty-seven I was the youngest senior executive in the history of Thalhimer Brothers, Inc., which, at that time, numbered nineteen stores! My salary doubled as the dust gathered on my flute.

My brother, Fred, had purchased our uncle's dry cleaning business about this time. Our mother was thrilled that her 'boys' were successful businessmen. Fred and I were both growing up and, as adults, had drifted apart temporarily. He and I were to become best of friends in later life. I was able to accomplish one thing during this period of my life that I look back on as of monumental significance. In Richmond, Virginia, the 1960s were tumultuous times. Racial integration was in full swing. At first, many Virginians opposed this new and radical idea of racial equality. My assuming the duties of Manager and Buyer meant the Assistant Buyer position was vacant and needed to be filled. To set the stage more accurately, let me say that in addition to my duties from 8am to 6pm five days a week, I was taking a correspondence course from the Gemmological Institute of America in the study of diamonds. I also took a part-time job as Choir Director at a Southern Baptist church in South Richmond. I thrived on directing the choir. It was a good choir and we usually did a good job of our Sunday performances. An assistant was something I needed desperately! I was very over-extended.

I was instrumental in the store promoting an African-American lady, Elizabeth Billups, to the Assistant Buyer position within the Silver and Jewellery Departments. She was the very first person of colour to work in a managerial and executive position in the store's long history. I like to think that I helped open the door for the policy Thalhimers would later adopt as an Equal Opportunity Employer. Elizabeth's was not a political promotion! She had worked for many years in the Silver Department behind the scenes as a clerical person.

In the early 1990s, Thalhimer Bros. Department Stores, Inc. went out of business, due in part to the advent of shopping malls and mega retailers such as Wal-Mart and Best Products. Retailing changed drastically during these years as did changing demographics and tastes of the American people. Often what had been traditional became an object of scorn. America's 'old line' traditional department stores were a relict of the past. They are mourned by many as an important facet of American life of a quieter, more genteel and refined time. The era of 'Big Is Better' and foreign imports was just emerging. The Mom and Pop retail establishment, of which Thalhimers was an example, was on the way out.

Balancing all this with fairly regular flights to New York City on buying trips, there was precious little free time. The flute stayed in its case and gathered more dust. I philosophised that the difference between a professional and an amateur musician was that a professional played for money and an amateur played for the love of music. As inaccurate as that may be, it brought solace to me during these artistically desolate times.

One day I decided to escape all this by enrolling in R.P.I. as a graduate composition major. I called the school and made an appointment with my old mentor, Milton Cherry. During the time in Germany, I had composed a quintet for flute and strings written in the Schoenberg Twelve Tone System. Since it was written for Lillian, in honour of her birth, I gave the handwritten score and parts to her recently. She did not seem overly impressed. Why should she have been? It was 2006.

After the usual handshake and a bit of catching up with what was going on in our lives, I recall Mr Cherry relating to me that his youngest child, Ann, had been ill and, by the way, was becoming quite a good flutist. I explained to Milton that I had a burning desire to study composition with him. I left the handwritten score of the quintet with Milton for him and the committee to study.

Milton Cherry contacted me shortly thereafter and asked me to come over to the Music School for a chat. We sat down in his dishevelled office with the familiar electric coffee pot, open violin case and cigarette butts scattered everywhere, a large bust of Beethoven glaring fiercely over the mess. Fiddle music was scattered everywhere. I was home again! Milton was one to get straight to the point without any sugar coating. He said to me, "Bob, we have examined the score of yours and the faculty has come to the conclusion that you are either a genius or a complete idiot." He went on, "Whichever you are, we have agreed that you will be accepted as a graduate student in composition." I thanked him profusely, knowing that my family and job responsibilities left no time for further schooling. I think Milton Cherry knew that too, and the matter was never broached again. Sadly, that was to be the last time I saw him.

The recently acquired choir-directing job at Bethany Place Baptist Church proved to be an important musical milestone and outlet for me. It provided me my first opportunity to do some choral conducting. To this point, my only conducting experience had been at R.P.I. I discovered not only did I love directing, but I was a fairly decent conductor.

My entrance into the Methodist ministry was facilitated by Dr A. Purnell Bailey, the District Superintendent of the

Richmond District in 1964. He was one of the more prominent figures of Virginia Methodism for decades. Dr Bailey, the author of *Our Daily Bread*, a nationally syndicated devotional column, died two or three years ago. My father's first comment to me when I told him of my plan was that I would have to quit smoking – which I did not do, and to this day I enjoy smoking a custom blend of Dunhill Tobacco in one of my Petersen Pipes. I am certain, as I look back, the poor man was fearful that I would make a mess out of the church, or worse still, be an embarrassment to him in his position of elder statesman of the Virginia Conference. At the time he was on the verge of retirement. His record was beyond reproach and I think he wanted to keep it that way. I would like to interject at this point that my father and I grew closer as time went on. His death at age ninety-five was the most heart-wrenching event of my life. To this day I miss him very much.

On September 28, 1964, an important event took place and the direction of our lives would be changed forever. On September 28, 1964, the Hawkins family was blessed by another addition, this time a bouncing baby boy we named Thomas. He, along with his older sister, Lillian, was not only a blessing, but also created for us some subtle changes in lifestyle. I matriculated at Wesley Theological Seminary located in our nation's capital. The year I spent at Wesley Seminary enabled me to spend a great deal more time with the children and Ann. When he was eighteen months old, we discovered through a routine doctor's visit that Tommy had a congenital heart defect. Close monitoring through his childhood and adolescence and on into adult life was necessary. When Tommy was in his thirties, he received open-heart surgery and is now better than new.

My thirty-five year career as a United Methodist Minister had begun. During this first year of seminary, I served a small, rural church in Caroline County. I never once recall my wife, Ann, complaining or making a negative comment. She stayed home and reared the children with not much help from me during this early period. One important character trait of Ann's was her fabulous sense of humour. She was funny! I mean that in the highest and most complimentary sense. I am persuaded it was her sense of humour that enabled her to survive with a smile during these years. I became dissatisfied with Wesley Seminary, as well as living in the metropolitan Washington DC area, and commuting sixty miles one way to Wrights Chapel once or twice a week. I was fed up with the entire 'ball of wax'. The seminary was too modern, not enough good old mouldy theology! DC was a nightmare – the traffic was horrible. The commute to the church, even though gas was about 30 cents a gallon, was breaking the bank. I had a very small bank!

It was during this brief time that Ann and I made friends with John and Irene Swisher. John's quick wit and wisdom made him delightful company. He had, without a doubt, one of the deepest philosophical minds I ever encountered, as well as being a man of inordinate generosity. Ann, the children and I spent many a Sunday after services at Wright's Chapel having dinner with John and Irene. John was a television repairman and dealer. His rural shop on US Route 1 at Ladysmith was the scene of many a relaxing weekend for us. John and his brother David became avid motorcycle enthusiasts. One thing about my friend John – he never paid anyone to fix anything! He would find a way to do it himself. John died of a heart attack in the 1990s. I conducted his funeral service in Caroline County in the Wright's Chapel Cemetery. I buried John in close proximity to his TV Shop where he worked and lived with Irene in an apartment over the shop. That has all been demolished now to make room for inevitable progress. Or is it? David, John's younger brother, and I have stayed in touch to the present. At age seventy-eight, David is the proud holder of the most miles travelled award on a BMW motorcycle. In 2005, BMW (North America) gave him this top mileage award for having ridden over 1,200,000 miles on BMW motorcycles. My own entrance into the world of motorcycling was to begin in 1972, a few years 'down the road', so to speak.

In 1965 an event took place that would reshape my life. The bishop, under divine inspiration (I hope), sent me and my little family of four to Gum Spring Methodist Church located – where else but? – Gum Spring, Virginia. Looking back on my ministry, I can say without reservation that the years of 1967 through 1971 were among the happiest we ever spent.

After such a long hiatus, I was finally able to return to the flute. I was comfortably able to practise each day. It took a surprisingly short time to recoup my playing to a reasonable level of proficiency. I conclude playing the flute is similar to riding a bicycle. Once you learn, you never forget. You just have to become re-acquainted. Then too, unlike a bicycle, one seldom falls off his or her flute. Lillian had reached the age of five and I was certain she was to be the next generation's Paula Robison. I gave my darling daughter flute lessons, impressed upon her that a minimum of one hour a day was required to play the flute (and please her father). I made many mistakes in my life. Expecting a five-year-old to have the same motivation as a student at Julliard was not only foolish on my part, but very unfair to little Lillian. She studied with me for about seven years. During these years the three of us gave little recitals, Lillian and me on flutes, her mother at the piano. As I reflect on my own immaturity and selfishness, I can see now that I put this adorable child in the position to feel that playing the flute was how she gained her father's love. Nothing could have been further from the truth. How is a five-year-old to know this?

But I admit, I was proud of my daughter's musical talent! In the fifth grade, Lillian was asked to play principal flute with the local high school band in their Christmas Concert! I have a picture of the band – her feet didn't touch the floor! This was, I think, the year we gave a serious and demanding recital in the church. I had given Lillian a sterling silver Gemeinhardt open hole flute. She, her mother and I gave a recital which included Domenico Cimarosa's *Concerto for Two Flutes* as well as a Haydn *Trio*. My memory of this could not be sharper had it been yesterday. Lillian played the second part to the Cimarosa *Concerto* impeccably!

It would be many years later, 2004 to be exact, that I would play this concerto again. The second flutist was fairly accomplished, but he made hash out of the part. I remembered my little Lillian and her wonderful playing many years before, and tears came to my eyes.

A short time later, Lillian would tell me with downcast eyes that she was going to give up the flute. Needless to say, my first thought was to send her to Virginia's finest psychiatrist for therapy. In her wisdom, she conveyed to me that she loved me very much, but didn't love the flute. I realized that this was a good trade-off. I suppose it was this experience of Lillian's that saved Tommy from being 'force fed' a musical instrument. Knowing him, he would have wanted to play the bass drum.

Not long ago Lillian, at age forty-two or so and the mother of two teenagers, asked me why I had allowed her to stop playing the flute. My response was something like, "Honey, you are the mother of two adolescent members of our species; you know the answer!"

To return to Gum Spring: this was my first full-time, genuine experience as a pastor of a church. When I say full-time, I mean my workload was full-time. In addition to serving the church during these four years, I attended Union Theological Seminary in Virginia. Past studies in music, such as theory, counterpoint and music history, came fairly easy to me. I confess that seminary was quite different. Union Seminary, being Presbyterian and wed to the Westminster Confession, required all students to study New Testament Greek as well as Hebrew. The idea was that a theologian preacher should be able to exegete the scriptures in their original language. The merits of this are debatable. During this period of my life, I spent my time studying, preaching, visiting the sick and sinful, attending a fine seminary, enjoying my role as husband and father as well as playing the flute again. There are many, many little stories I could tell. Suffice it to say that this time at Gum Spring gave us a firm grounding in family as well as community values. I enjoyed preaching and conducting corporate worship. I also was certain that the Almighty enjoyed my flute playing, and would provide ample opportunity for music in my life in the future.

As all good things must come to an end, so did our time at Gum Spring. During this time, ministers remained in one church or appointment an average of four years. The powers that be, defined as the bishop and his cabinet of superintendents, saw fit to send us to a town I had never heard of – *Victoria*. Victoria is an old railroad town in rural Southside Virginia. At that time it was suffering mightily from the merger of the Norfolk and Western Railway with the Virginian Railway. Unemployment among railroad men was extraordinarily high. The entire economy was adversely affected since the railroad was the largest single employer in Victoria. For three years I worked among townspeople who were in an economic crunch: individuals and families who were seeing the American Dream vaporize before their eyes. Life in Victoria was not a happy time. Ann also found this time to be one to forget. For the first time since we met, I recognized discontent and sadness on her part. The smile was fading. The laughter was not vibrant anymore.

I needed a miracle, badly. And a miracle, second only to the change of Army orders in the middle of the Atlantic, happened in the spring of 1974. One of the finest gentlemen of the Virginia Methodist, Carroll Freeman, my superintendent on the Farmville District where Victoria was located, was to retire. He made it known that he wanted me to be his preacher in retirement. This meant that after three years of suffering in Victoria, God had paroled us and was to send us to Blackstone, or the 'promised land!' It was as if by Divine Providence we were lifted from the depths of darkness into the light of eternal bliss! (I'm allowed to talk like this; after all, I *am* a man of the cloth!). I was eager and certain this would be my most enjoyable and meaningful pastorate. Crenshaw Church had a pipe organ as well as central air conditioning! I had arrived at my 'medieval music conservatory' that served also as a church.

The church I was to serve had a long-standing reputation for its fine music programme. In June of 1974, the Hawkins family drove to Blackstone. Here begins one of the shortest, yet most fascinating chapters of my ministry. The first day I went to the church and arranged my office, unpacking my fairly impressive library of theological books and arranging them on the bookshelves of my spacious and well-appointed office. The church treasurer called for an appointment for that afternoon. At the appointed time the treasurer arrived and introduced himself to me. He took a seat across from my desk. I felt uncomfortable behind the desk, and took a chair facing the treasurer.

He was a fine older gentleman in his fifties. He proceeded to tell me that the church's choir director/organist was away for the summer studying for his Master of Music degree at Westminster Choir College in New York. He would be returning to Blackstone in a week or less. In the meantime, he said, he thought I should be made aware that the choir director had charged large amounts of money on music at various music stores and publishing houses in the name of the church. It seemed that there was an unbudgeted sum in excess of $800 owed by the church. I was asked to handle the problem as tactfully as I could. I assured this good man he had nothing to worry about. He left me with a number of unpaid invoices to serve as grist for my first meeting with our very talented, if not fiscally responsible, church musician. I realized the seriousness of the situation, but confess I was amused by what could have turned into a disaster of monumental proportion.

The Director of Music Ministries was ushered into my office, and I was determined he would make a full accounting of the error of his ways. He turned out to be not only one of the best organist/directors in Virginia Methodism, but one of the most personable and likable people I ever met. I explained, as best I could without hurting his feelings, the church's position. I asked for an explanation. He was very upfront with me, and apologetically told me much of the music he had bought for his and his wife's private lessons in their home. I asked him to please never do anything like this again. He was a bit surprised when I told him there were no more charge accounts in stores in Virginia, and in the future, any music ordered in the church's name had to be approved by me. This ended forever the problems of the church's music budget.

Life in Blackstone was busy, exciting and fulfilling. The children seemed happy, Lillian became a pompom girl in middle school and Tommy had the happiest two years of his life – both in the fourth grade! His teacher, Miss Williams, loved him, but she held his feet to the fire. I must admit Tommy never exhibited great scholarly interest. Ann easily made friends and was involved in the musical life of the church. At Christmas the choir performed the Christmas Section of Handel's *Messiah*. Ann played the organ for the performance. She did a good job and practised untold hours. She took organ lessons from our friend, the church organist and director. The same Christmas, the church staged Menotti's *Amahl and the Night Visitors*. I was to do the part of King Balthazar. To put on both of these major musical undertakings was a Herculean task!

Aside from the musical life, I was deeply involved in the administration of the church which had been ignored in past years. The people of both the church and town were very receptive to my leadership. To this day, Lillian's best friend is a young lady who went to middle school with her. For Ann it was different; she put on a happy face, but her personal problems were getting the better of her. Life for Ann at this time was stressful in the extreme, both mentally and physically. She was hospitalised for a few weeks and this frightened me more than anyone knew, then or now. We had a lot of emotional debris to clean up.

Our friend, the choir director, and his wife received an offer to go to a large church in Roanoke, Virginia. I was devastated, as was the congregation of our church. I had visions of Crenshaw Church's music programme becoming just like most other churches in Southside Virginia. This was not to happen! A young man, James Carmichael, the brother of the wife of our former director, applied for the job and was hired on the spot. He is a fine organist and years later was to become one of the top organists in San Francisco, California.

Under his direction the music programme soared. He and I became close friends and developed a mutual respect.

During my pastorate in Blackstone and associations with these fine musicians, the flute once again became a prominent part of my life. The church had, in addition to a fine organ, a grand piano and a harpsichord. I recall a wedding in the church in which we played a Sonata by Marcello for flute and harpsichord prior to the processional. The people of the church seemed very pleased to have a flute-playing pastor, and very supportive of my involvement in the church's music ministry. Many a Sunday's Service was opened by music for flute and organ or harpsichord. I fancied myself as some kind of modern Vivaldi, the 'Musician Priest'.

The bishop visited the church one day in 1976 and told me I was being moved to Culpeper United Methodist Church in Culpeper, Virginia, that June. I felt Ann and the children would benefit from living in a more cosmopolitan area. Culpeper is now considered a part of Northern Virginia and the metropolitan Washington DC megapolis. Then too, the church was much larger, roughly thirteen hundred members; it had a dynamic ministry and music programme. Should I also mention the salary was quite a bit higher? Yes, mundane things like salary are important, even to men of the cloth!

So it was to be, in June of 1976 after just two wonderful years in Blackstone, my family and I once again moved the piano from the living room to the moving van for a trip across the State of Virginia to our new church and adventure. The Hawkins family was full of anticipation. The children were less than happy over moving away from their friends. "You will make new ones," Ann told them. We pulled out the driveway a little after twelve noon. Our plan was to stop in Ladysmith and spend the night with the Swishers.

Chapter 7 (Ann)

(1978 – 2001)

After my marriage broke up I threw myself into everything imaginable. Big businessmen decided to build a short-take-off-and-landing airport a mile or so from my house, in a very built-up area of East London. I wrote to the local newspaper criticizing the choice of location, and the paper made a big thing of my letter. Some local people, who had formed a committee to fight the airport, contacted me and suddenly I found myself involved in local politics. Well, very local – I doubt the Labour Party knew we existed! As the only educated person on the committee, I was made secretary. I don't remember all the members anymore, but the Chair was a lovely lady (Connie) whose house, when the STOLport was built, was right beside the runway. There is a special way of communicating among the Eastenders which I never understood: they would speak in half sentences, never bothering to complete a statement; yet, they all knew what they meant. Except me. I never understood the language of the semi-sentence. But I loved the people. They were outspoken but honest, and always there if you needed help. It made me proud to be accepted into this community.

    We lost our fight, of course. But it's a small airport and planes don't go or come all the time. In fact, where I lived it made no difference. Connie, on the other hand, had the planes' headlights shining into her sitting room.

Another avenue I explored was the world of psychic phenomena. I studied mediumship and spiritual healing at the College of Psychic Studies. I never managed to become any kind of medium, although I did get some things right; the law of averages, I suspect. I met some wonderful people interested in the spiritual aspects of music, and two truly great souls: Geoff Boltwood and Keith Casburn. They both made a deep impression on my life, and Keith especially supported me when I later developed Parkinson's disease.

I actually dated a medium for a while, a man I met at a psychic forum, but he failed to foresee that I was going to dump him. He was a male chauvinist pig and I am mortified that I let him browbeat me – to the extent that when I broke a bone in my foot and was told by the doctor not to use it, I still cooked his dinner. I went for a couple of counselling sessions to work up the courage to tell him to get lost. One day, shortly after we broke up, my neighbours informed me that Ivor had dropped by while I was at work and 'borrowed' my iron. I had the locks changed immediately and sure enough, he stopped by the next day, presumably to borrow something else. Ha! He couldn't get in!

In the mid-seventies, I was giving regular concerts with guitarist Bill Grandison and pianist Raphael Terroni. Bill and I did the rounds of the guitar societies, and with Ray (Raphael) I did not only recitals, but also gigs with Richard Baker – in those days probably the BBC's most noted newsreader. Ray was his regular pianist. Richard did an interesting mixture of entertainment: some readings, some songs. I played the *Carnival of Venice* (the Briccialdi version) in the Fairfield Hall – a very big and very full hall – wearing the most amazing period dress provided by the BBC. I was still married to Charlie when I did that gig. Oh yes, I also played with a couple of avant-garde ensembles. And, of course, I was still teaching at Trinity College of Music; the London College of Music eventually offered me the post of Head of Woodwind. The government had brought in pay reforms by this time, and the salary at TCM jumped to £8 an hour. The LCM also raised its pay, but not quite to that extent.

Teaching is never dull! One of my LCM pupils, an Irish boy, got picked up for being drunk and disorderly. The police beat him up. They literally threw him in the back of a van and tweaked him in ways that were painful but left no marks. A bystander was taking photographs of the police brutality and the officers took his camera and broke it. I had to appear in court as a character witness. As supportive as I am of the police, it was obvious they had overreacted. The judge said as much, but since my pupil had filed a counter-suit against the police, the judge found Aiden guilty, with a suspended sentence. Aiden went to America and the last I heard was conducting his own orchestra.

Another pupil, a TCM student this time, accepted a dare to get on the underground without a ticket. London Transport made an example of her. I wasn't required to appear in court this time; I had only to write a letter to the court on her behalf, which was read out loud. She was so obviously a nice girl that London Transport looked a little silly trying to make her a criminal type. We're still in touch.

Speaking of public transport, I remember one recital Ray and I did in Nottingham, north of London. We were on the train and it broke down. We sat on the tracks for three hours and arrived at the concert venue with the audience already seated. There went our rehearsal – out the window! We changed clothes and played cold. But it went well.

Ray lived south of London and I drove my Kawasaki 250 to his house for rehearsals. It was a pleasant journey in the summer, but in the winter my hands would take close to an hour to return to life! I have wondered if that is one reason I developed tendon problems in my left hand.

Oh, yes – Richard Baker took me to Scotland and Belfast. That was scary! – playing the *Carnival of Venice* on James Galway's home territory.

In 1991, the London College of Music got deeply in debt. The school was situated on a prime site near Oxford Circus, but it was an old building and needed a lot of maintenance. That was just one of the financial worries. Members of the staff formed an association to try to help save the college, to keep it independent, but the staff association was not encouraged by the management. For some unknown reason, we were seen as a threat. The staff's main interest was in saving their jobs and the conservatory, and the board members' prime consideration appeared to lie in not becoming personally liable for a million pound debt. The LCM was not a limited company at this point, the solicitor not having at this time sent in the necessary papers.

The LCM, a unique establishment in many ways, began life in 1887 and grew into a full music college complete with a Saturday school for children. When I joined the staff in 1975, William Lloyd Webber – father of Andrew and Julian Lloyd Webber – was the Principal. He was a warm and caring man and under his guidance the LCM thrived. I performed his *Sonatina* for flute and piano at the college, a work written, he told me, while bombs were falling on London. Yet the music displays a remarkable lightness of character – really, the *Sonatina* is a musical metaphor for the courage of the British people during a horrible time. Lloyd Webber remained Director of the LCM from 1964 until his death in

1982. If my memory is correct, he was succeeded by composer John McCabe.

Some of my most interesting pupils came through the LCM, and it was a sad day when it finally closed its doors as an independent establishment and merged with Thames Valley University. There may have been a chance that Andrew Lloyd Webber might have considered joining the fight to keep the college independent, but the way I heard it, the board decided not to enlist his help because his was the 'wrong type of music'. How ridiculous!

The space TVU allocated to the music school consisted of a few rooms on the ground floor for offices and class teaching, and for instrumental lessons we were given basement rooms with no soundproofing. Invariably, when I wanted to teach tone production to a fairly quiet flautist, there would be a trumpet and piano rehearsal in the next room!

In an effort to keep the name of the LCM alive and distinct from the University, I started a woodwind quintet made up of professorial staff. We gave concerts at festivals and institutions in and around London. The mayor of Slough frequently came to our performances. The bottom half of the quintet was simply amazing: Anthony Randall on horn and Brian Blackwood on bassoon – two of England's finest musicians.

The LCM was known for its homosexual-friendly atmosphere. For many years two of the men in important managerial positions were gays. When the LCM merged with TVU, its homosexual contingent increased and, at this point, it (sexual freedom) began to be abused. One of my students came to me, very upset, because a member of management was making advances to him. It's silly, isn't it, what we call sexual freedom. If my pupil had been female and a teacher or other personnel made a pass at her, the teacher would have been severely rebuked and possibly dismissed. But because the pupil was male, he had nowhere to go to complain – unless he went to the very people who were harassing him! I went to see the Vice-Chancellor of the University and told him the story, but I also had to tell him my pupil wouldn't admit it in public. The Vice-Chancellor said he would keep an eye on the situation, which he did, and the offender was soon dismissed. It's the only time in my life I have been a tell-tale; but I believe young boys should have the same protection as young girls.

But the saddest thing of all to do with the merger was the bloodbath that ensued among the LCM staff members. Several people saw the merger as a chance to further their careers and didn't care who was destroyed in the process. One woman in particular stepped on her friends. It was nasty. I walked out.

While I'm on the subject of music schools, Trinity College of Music was also having financial worries and the Board decided not to renew the lease on the building where most of the instrumental teaching took place. We went through a very tense time while various options and mergers were discussed, but TCM was more transparent than the LCM, and the management was reasonably good at sharing their thinking with the staff. Eventually, a decision to relocate to Greenwich was made. I took early retirement because of illness the year Trinity moved.

During the last few years of my time at Trinity, I was chairperson of our local branch of NATFHE (National Association of Teachers in Further and Higher Education). I had to deal with matters between staff and management. Egos were what I really had to deal with – little people in little positions in the little world of one little institution, each thinking s/he was better than the next and many having hidden agendas. I have to say that it was as hard to work with members of the NATFHE committee as it was with TCM's management. My first secretary had a severe drinking problem. In addition to his work at TCM, he directed a church choir in the centre of London. At one rehearsal, he went amok and started throwing choir books at the singers. But I preferred him to his replacement, who was a scaremonger and secretive, and full of his own self-importance.

The management made no effort to disguise the fact that they considered the teaching staff to be suffered only because you couldn't have a school without them. But occasionally the union had some success. We got a nice settlement for one teacher who had become mentally ill.

Chapter 8 (Bob)

(1975 - 1985)

Our arrival in Culpeper was exciting. The church, set atop a hill, overlooked an upscale residential neighbourhood. The rolling Blue Ridge Mountains could be seen in the distance. The Church Office consisted of a suite of offices – mine had its own private lavatory. I had 'arrived!'

My delight was short-lived; it wasn't long before I discovered that this was the most difficult church I had ever served. One Sunday, an anonymous letter was placed on the pulpit. I read it aloud to the congregation. You could have heard a pin drop! Looking back objectively, we were certainly not the usual parsonage family. Tommy, at age fourteen, was arrested for breaking into the church. I went to the police station and raised hell and the trumped up charges were dropped. Ann and the children came under close scrutiny. My motorcycle and moustache were grist for criticism. Yet my pulpit presence and preaching never came under fire. In fact, nothing related to the work of a pastor was criticized.

After dinner one evening, I left home to attend what I thought was to be an official committee meeting. I was told that they – the committee (also known as the 'powers that be') – would concern themselves with the financial matters of he church, and for me to 'stick to matters of religion!' The meeting adjourned and I walked home in the crisp cool mountain air of the evening and prayed. I was to learn, in short order, just who the movers and shakers were in the church and city. Ann, for the first time in her life, took a job with a local bank as a teller. I think it is fair to say that the Culpeper Church was not the centre of my family's life – just mine.

At this time in my life I was riding a BMW motorcycle, an act which was not well received by some members of this church. This was the first church I ever served that did not receive my hobby of motorcycling with open minds, if not open hearts! My moustache was also a problem with some of the more traditional parishioners. I am certain now, in retrospect, I was as much a challenge to them as they were to me.

The church's organist and choir director was a young man of considerable talent. He owned a very fine harpsichord and he and I would perform recitals and chamber music concerts with a violinist who was a member of the church. From the outset, my flute stayed as busy as there was time to give to music. As the pastor of one of the more prestigious churches in Virginia, I was called upon to serve on various State or Conference committees. I accepted the challenge and found myself driving all over Virginia doing 'connectional' work. What time that was left was shared between the church, my family and music. I confess that all suffered as there were only twenty-four hours in a day. I was becoming tired, depressed and restless. I exhibited classic symptoms of burn-out.

Choral directing, of all things, presented itself as balm for my sad, sick soul. Culpeper had a Chorale Society of long standing. I was invited to become the director, and I readily accepted. I rehearsed and directed their musical ensemble for three years in Culpeper. Occasionally Ann would play to accompany the group in concert. I was especially pleased that Lillian elected to sing with us.

The church kept me busy with administration, service and sermon preparation as well as counselling, hospital and home visitation. Study and sermon preparation, out of sheer necessity, was sandwiched in between everything else. Much time was spent visiting new residents to this rapidly growing area. During those three years I received an average of one-hundred-and-twenty newcomers into the church's membership each year. There were great expectations in those days for the minister to visit his flock regularly. If I may say so myself, I did an admirable job of most of these things! I found relief from the rigours of church life by visiting John and David Swisher in Ladysmith. It was a good cycle ride from Culpeper to Ladysmith on an occasional Saturday.

Not long into my pastorate here, I quite innocently stumbled onto one of the church's dark secrets! There was a special fund, supported for some twenty-five years through donations, to provide scholarships for deserving local college students. Upon examination of the records, I was mystified to learn that the church had never awarded a scholarship from this fund. The principal grew and interest increased. The lengths that the financial people and the trustees went to in order to hide and not spend any of this scholarship fund were astonishing. I was then, and am now, persuaded that a church, if it is true to the New Testament model, practises honesty, openness, kindness and charity. None of these qualities were very apparent to me as I looked at the 'powers that *were*'.

There are always numerous stories a minister can tell of experiences in the local church. One such story involves a dear elderly lady eighty-five years of age. From time to time I visited Mary and we would indulge in one of her vices. She had two: drinking a small glass of fine wine before bedtime; the other, smoking an occasional cigarette. Often I would sit with her and we would smoke a cigarette together. One day I received a telephone call informing me that dear Mary had been taken to the local hospital. I visited her the next day. The diagnosis was stomach cancer. Later I visited Mary in her home. She was depressed; she would hardly carry on a conversation with me. I asked her what was wrong. Mary said, "Reverend, the doctor told me I had to give up drinking wine and smoking cigarettes. If I didn't, it would kill me very soon." I concluded that at her age, if she lived a few more years happily smoking and drinking a few ounces of wine at night, what was the harm? We talked about it and she decided on her own with no coaching from me, that she would much rather live to eighty-seven happily than live to ninety miserably.

I excused myself, went to the store and bought the best bottle of wine they had. On my return to Mary's, we toasted each other and had a prayer and a cigarette. Mary lived three more years. I read of her demise after moving from Culpeper. I smiled, recalling Mary's happy state when I left her home after our 'party'. I concluded that neither the *Westminster Confession* nor the beloved *United Methodist Discipline* specifically forbade what I did. It was with a bit of spiritual grace that I recalled the words of Holy Writ that say, 'A little wine is good for the stomach'. In Mary's case, that would be good – very good! However, the question that begs answering philosophically, theologically, as well as with good old fashion 'horse sense' – was Mary's humanity served positively or negatively by my being her pastor?

In my second year in the Culpeper Church, the kingpin of Culpeper and I were to discover that the town and church were too small for the both of us. Having lived there for the greater part of his seventy-four years, he was not about to acquiesce to this young upstart of a preacher. He and his arch hatchet man, a retired pharmacist, told me there was a meeting Monday at 7:30pm and for me not to be late. The meeting was attended by only the three of us. It was about their personal desires, masked as the 'Committee's desires', detailing all the terrible things I had either done, or was going to do. They hated my long hair and moustache, hated my motorcycle, and generally just hated me. The problem was, for them, that the majority of the membership liked me, loved my preaching and my pastoral care. Their concern was really my meddling in the church's finances. The scholarship fund was their pet and they saw my making their stewardship of it public ending their total dictatorship of the purse strings of the church. I thanked them kindly for their support and adjourned the so-called meeting with an impassioned prayer.

The seeming mishandling of funds by a small group of men in the church caused me to take this to the district superintendent since it was too serious a problem for me to solve alone. The superintendent, who will go unidentified out of respect for the office, told me to ignore this and not 'rock the boat'. I then went to the resident bishop of the Conference and asked his opinion. Bishop Goodson replied, and I quote, "Bob, your church's actions are disgraceful, as well as dishonest and unchristian!" I thanked Bishop Goodson for his opinion which gave me a renewed faith in the Church. After three years as pastor of Culpeper Church, it became apparent that a change was in order. I needed something totally different. I wanted to serve a church that was a model of what I envisioned the Body of Christ to be.

In June of 1979, the Conference met and, again, the Lord and the bishop were led to send me and my family to Richmond, Virginia. I was certain Divine Providence had a hand in Methodism. Also, Ann could easily transfer her state job to Richmond, the home office. I was sent to serve Pace

Memorial United Methodist Church, which was to be the pinnacle of my ministry. In addition, my career as a recorder player would begin and flourish during these years in Richmond. My ministry was varied in this church. A staid, old downtown church, Pace Memorial had burned to the ground in 1968. Against the wishes of the Virginia Conference, a band of sturdy and stalwart Methodists rebuilt the church on the same small plot of ground at 700 West Franklin Street.

Pace Church had become a centre of refuge for the homeless, disinherited and disenfranchised in the inner city of Richmond. On the campus of Virginia Commonwealth University (formerly Richmond Professional Institute), the church was made up of a cadre of loyal Methodists from all over the city, as well as being the centre for the ecumenical United Campus Ministry. I established the Drop-In Center for the homeless and less fortunate of God's children. The congregation was multi-racial, multi-ethnic and multi-national. On any Sunday, we were about one-third white, a third African-American and the remainder looked like a gathering at the United Nations. Pace Church composed its own creed. It opened with these words, 'We believe in a color-blind God who made technicolor people.' In the spirit of love and compassion, Pace Church organized the only *Gay Alcoholic Anonymous* Chapter I know of.

A black student university activity, the *Black Awakening Choir*, rehearsed in the sanctuary one evening a week and sang for worship services one Sunday each month. On the surface, all was looking up for the Hawkins family. There were here no *powers that were*; it was a vibrant, faithful and committed congregation with a mission! In any given week, the church, students and I served a hundred or so hot meals to the homeless and hungry! On a few occasions, I brought homeless street-people home with me when the weather was cold and wet, otherwise they may have fallen victim to hypothermia. This was a 'leap of faith', housing some of Richmond's homeless, drug-addicted, alcoholic and downtrodden in the parsonage with my family. We never gave it a second thought.

However, these years in Richmond were not healthy ones for our family. Ann was working in a demanding job for the State of Virginia. Lillian had elected not to attend college, but rather had embarked on a career working for the state, a job which eventually grew into a very responsible faculty-level position at the College of William and Mary in Williamsburg, Virginia. I was immersed in the life of the church, as well as my musical endeavours. There was precious little time spent as a family. I have some huge regrets about this.

It was in this unlikely environment that my musical fortunes were to take a sharp turn and a new direction was charted. I had begun playing the recorder in 1979. The utter fascination with the soprano recorder soon was to include the alto recorder. And this church required unusual hours from me, usually afternoons and evenings. In the mornings Tommy was in school and Ann and Lillian were at work. I spent the morning hours at home practising the recorder. It came very easily and naturally to me. In just a year I was a pretty good recorder player! I gave two recitals in Savannah, Georgia. One, at Christ Episcopal Church, was broadcast on the local National Public radio station. I was asked to return later for another recital of Baroque recorder music and to lead a masterclass for the Savannah Recorder Society. To my surprise, the Sunday edition of the local newspaper had included a full-page article on my pending recital, and a pretty good write up on me and the recorder. Both of these musical programmes had Sue Guerry playing the harpsichord. Sue was, at that time, the keyboard player with the Savannah

Symphony Orchestra. She was an accomplished performer and impeccable musician. We were to team-up the coming year to present an Alumni Recital at Virginia Commonwealth University in Richmond.

I had joined forces with a group of early music enthusiasts in Richmond. With these new-found colleagues, many solo and chamber music programmes were given throughout the Greater Richmond metropolitan area. All of the major solo and chamber music venues in the city invited me, as a soloist or member of a chamber group, to perform. At this particular time, I was entrenched in the musical life of the city; Ann was climbing the ladder of professional success; Lillian had been given a series of promotions with the state; and Tommy graduated from Thomas Jefferson High School where he distinguished himself in the Dramatic Arts. Our family members went in separate directions, each doing his or her own thing. This was not a recipe for a healthy family.

I was using my hands for many hours a day playing the recorder, as I had done for three decades with the clarinet. The right hand when playing the recorder (unlike the flute) is very similar to the position and movement of the thumb and first finger when playing the clarinet. I attribute this time that I spent playing the recorder, compounded with the years previously as a clarinettist, to be at least part of the cause years later of debilitating arthritis in both hands, and the end of my flute playing.

History does repeat itself, at least in the life of a United Methodist Minister. In June of 1982 my family and I were sent to rescue St Matthews United Methodist from the work of Satan, otherwise known as the former pastor. St Matthews is twenty miles west of Richmond at Rockville (a crossroads and a post office). The church was in a really lovely rural setting replete with a running brook and woods. The setting was wonderful.

Ann had, by this time, secured herself professionally in a mid-level position with the State of Virginia. Her office was in Richmond, which she was unwilling to leave. I made an appointment with the bishop to explain to him why I had to stay within the Greater Richmond area. I confess the leader of Virginia Methodism took a very uncharitable view of my situation. He waved his finger in my face and said, "Bob, you are putting your wife's career ahead of your ministry." I am happy to say that this policy has now dramatically changed and spouses' and children's needs and welfare are now given consideration in the appointment process.

My appointment to St Matthews Church was the bishop's way of teaching me a lesson. Punishment took its toll on both my bank account and my self-esteem. The salary was significantly less than I had earned previously. The church was a typical entry-level appointment. A young seminarian entering the ministry would have been happy with this appointment; at age forty-seven I felt betrayed by the Church. I realize now that I was angry with Ann for her intransient position with her job and unwillingness to move to a larger, better paying church with me. This, in some measure, precipitated my professional decline as well as my loss of faith in the hierarchy of my denomination, who I realized were 'vessels made of clay', just as I was.

I took over the responsibilities of this new, rural appointment. Ann commuted daily to her job in Richmond. Lillian and Tommy were living in Richmond, involved in their jobs and enjoying life in the city as young adults are prone to do. I relaxed by riding my motorcycle. Ann and I slowly drifted apart. We were too busy to notice.

Admittedly, I was no good to St Matthews Church, to myself or the ministry – certainly not as a father or husband.

In June 1983, Ann and I celebrated our twenty-fifth wedding anniversary. Shortly thereafter we were to separate. Ann moved out of the parsonage, back to her beloved Richmond. Lillian and Tommy were on their own – and so was I! There I was just me, my BMW and recorders (which I had lost interest in during this depressing period). Mental concentration was virtually impossible for me. I realize now that I was not far from a nervous breakdown.

The parsonage was empty. The ensuing months were the darkest and emptiest of my life. My devastation was made more severe knowing that much of the problem with my marriage was caused by me. I had been simply too busy. I had neglected Ann and the children in the guise of being a good pastor to my flock. The divorce was final in June of 1985. I rode the motorcycle to Savannah and visited Bob and Kitty Hill. The familiar surroundings there brought back too many memories. I left Savannah one morning at five o'clock. It was May, but I remember nearly freezing in the unusually chilly temperatures for this time of year as I rode the eight hours home.

The nest was really empty now, and I knew I was not created to live alone. The mileage on the motorcycle increased dramatically. During this period of depression and feelings of being abandoned, music was in no way a solace. The recorder sat idle, as I rode my motorcycle some fifteen thousand miles in ten months.

There was a young lady, a member of my church whose husband had served as pastor to this church, who had not attended since I had been the pastor. I knew she and her husband had been through a divorce, and that his actions had been thoroughly investigated by the Committee on Investigation of the Virginia Conference. Her name was brought to my attention when a mailing from the church was returned with her new address supplied by the U.S. Postal Service. As any conscientious minister would do, I called her and told her she was missed at her church. A few phone calls over the period of a week or so prompted my asking her to have dinner with me.

Martha John was the mother of a vibrant, energetic six-year-old, Elizabeth. Bett, as she was affectionately known, was to become a major part of my life. Martha John and I had a whirlwind courtship, lasting only from March until our October wedding. Going against all the conventional wisdom regarding 'jumping from the frying pan into the fire', I persevered.

I recall my father's seeming fear and trepidation upon my entering the ministry and understand why he felt as he did! I was beginning to share a little of his apprehension.

Martha and I settled on an October 6, 1985 wedding. I think this takes some explaining. The bishop had forbidden me to marry Martha John. He and I nearly engaged in fisticuffs in his office over my romantic plans. I told him he could not forbid me to marry. Her former husband had struck up a romantic relationship with the church's secretary; they were discovered by members of the church. For this reason, bad publicity and the possibility of more bad press, the good bishop was furious with me, threatened all manner of retribution, as well as the possibility of Divine judgment. I left the bishop's office determined to become an orchestral flutist – if any orchestra would have me. Maybe the Barnum and Bailey Circus Band needed a piccolo player? That, even in these dire straits, was too desperate to even consider!

Then one day in September, Bishop Blackburn called me. In a friendly and sincere tone, he told me of a fine church in Lawrenceville, Virginia that was in need of a pastor by Thanksgiving to replace their pastor who was on medical leave with heart trouble. He went on to say that I would be a perfect choice for this larger church, except they needed a family in their parsonage. He asked me, "Martha John has a small daughter, doesn't she? Bob, could you and Martha John be married by November?"

I told the bishop I would see what I could do as I fought to stifle uncontrollable laughter. Martha was in New Orleans at a business seminar. I met her at the airport when she returned and casually asked her if she would like to get married. She replied happily, "Yes, when?"

"October 6," I replied sheepishly.

On the way home I explained the entire unexplainable scenario. We hugged and said to each other, "Let's do it!" Martha had a marvellous career in computers, as a programmer and data specialist dealing in organ transplants. She left a career and a salary more than double mine, and cast her lot as a preacher's wife – again!

Bett was the centre of attraction and omni-present. She was a fine student and could debate at an early age with the best. Years later, Bett was to graduate from college *magna cum laude.* Today, she is in her fifth year as a school teacher. At the time, I wondered if she would ever reach high school! Looking back, I understand why the Good Lord gives children to young people. I was fifty years old, and being a new parent of a small child was for me, difficult, to put it mildly.

We did not tell anyone other than our immediate families of our plans. We had a quiet ceremony at Martha's house in Richmond. A minister friend of ours officiated at the wedding ceremony written by the two of us, and attended by our close immediate family members. The 'Trust and Obey' part was omitted from the Order of Service for some reason that escapes me just now. Martha John and I left immediately after the wedding, aboard my motorcycle, to visit my parents in Kilmarnock. My parents became devoted to Martha John, and thanked her for 'saving their son's life'. Martha is a gifted mathematician and scientist. I am a theologian and musician. No two people could be so different. That was to prove a blessing as well as a curse.

Maybe you will conclude Martha John and I were having an affair while I was still married to Ann. Nothing could be further from the truth. From today's vantage point, it matters little to me – other than a truthful account. The fact is, I didn't meet Martha John until after my separation from Ann.

By the way – she loved motorcycling and in the coming years, we were to see much of America's East Coast from the BMW. Martha John was my truest fan when it came to my music and my preaching. Her devotion to her husband's accomplishments was both sincere and remarkable. I readily confess I was proud to have married a lady with far superior gifts of intellect and social graces than I would ever possess. By her own admission, her musical talent comes up short.

The physical move from our church and community went smoothly, and the people of the Lawrenceville United Methodist Church welcomed the three of us, the newly weds plus one, into their parsonage, church and hearts in mid-November 1985.

Chapter 9 (Ann)

(1975 – 2008)

When my parents retired to England in 1975, it was their intention to live in a town house in London, but when they arrived here, having taken the huge step of selling their American property and many of their worldly goods, my mother was more than a little homesick. So, instead of settling down in London, they bought a house just outside Reading, which was like a smaller version of their home in Virginia. However, Mother had done her homework and knew where to find a town within easy commuting distance. In fact, she found she had to contact so many different agencies, both in the States and in England, to get the information she needed to relocate, that she combined it all in a book titled *Would You Like to Live in England?* To travel into London, they had to drive into Reading (there was only a once-an-hour bus on that route) and catch a train. The bus was infrequent but the trains were many and fast. My parents had a lot of fun when they first moved here. They played in an amateur orchestra, formed a string quartet and went to lots of concerts.

My parents came to some of my concerts, but my mother used to get so nervous that it made her ill. Unfortunately, she failed to hide her nerves, and that made me nervous. Suddenly music was not so much fun. It became hard work. After a while we tacitly agreed that they wouldn't come to my concerts. Mother's nerves were too hard on me. But the damage was done, and nerves became a reality in my performing career.

In the early eighties, Daddy began to show signs of Alzheimer's Disease. I would ride down to Burghfield Common (I was now riding a motorcycle with some oomph; I had taken two motorcycle courses by this time and could even do simple maintenance!) on the weekends and wash their dog, and do anything else that needed doing. And each time it would take Daddy longer to remember who I was. Mother was devastated. She was determined not to put him into a home, but she found herself living with a stupid old man instead of the dashing and witty violinist she had married. The doctor convinced her to put Daddy into a home for a couple of weeks to give her a break, and I stayed with her as much as my work commitments would allow. A year later she agreed to a second break, and this time, while Daddy was away, Mother had a bad fall. Something seemed to snap. She refused to walk again. Fortunately, it was the Christmas break and I was able to stay with her. The doctor told me to get her to walk, even if it was just around the bed.

"Oh, Ann!" Mom cried, "are you trying to kill me?"

While Daddy was in the home he suffered a brain haemorrhage and was taken to hospital. It was Christmas Eve and I tried to get Mother to go to the hospital with me, while she tried to get me to stay with her. In the end I went to be with Daddy. The nurse said I should go home and take care of Mother because Daddy didn't know who I was. My father died in the hospital, alone, on December 27, 1986.

It always surprised me that Mother never even thought about trying to get to the hospital. Now I can look back and see that to her, Daddy had already died. I will never forget the time, early on, when he leaned towards me and said, "I'm losing my mind, you know." I hope he didn't know it for long.

I don't know if Mother found life easier or more difficult after Daddy died. She was certainly miserable, and she rang me several times a day. She asked me to quit my teaching jobs, my main source of income, and live with her, and she would pay me a salary. Even if that had been a desirable proposition, there seemed no way to make such a plan work. If I gave up my teaching jobs, I would never get them back after Mother died. Good teaching positions are hard to find. It also felt like – and I think it was – a ploy to stop me from giving concerts. She refused to live with me in my house, and she was right; it was too tiny and she would never have managed the steep stairs. She occasionally hired a night nurse, which at least meant she was getting some help. She still refused to walk. My heart cries for her as I write this; she was so unhappy. I didn't know how to help her.

They say misery loves company, and that was certainly the case here. Every day, when I got home after teaching or rehearsing, there would be no fewer than five phone calls on my answerphone, all from my mother and all complaining. If a concert were looming, she would get sick and tell me I had to go to her instead. I went to see her at every opportunity, but frankly the whole situation was getting me down, too. For the only time in my life, I went on tranquillisers. I tried not telling her when I had a gig, but that didn't work because she telephoned me every couple of hours and was frantic if I didn't answer. I tried telling her in advance of a gig, and she would get ill. And that's how I eventually killed her. I was offered a chance to play a recital on TV, on the Arts Channel. This was a rare opportunity and if I turned it down, it was unlikely the offer would be repeated. I decided to tell Mother well in advance about this wonderful opportunity, to give her a chance to get used to the idea; I hoped enough remained of the musician inside her to give her support. Instead, she got very ill and went into hospital with terminal pneumonia. My sister came over from the USA to stay at the hospital with Mother while I did the recital. I'm glad to say that Mother lived long enough for me to get to the hospital, but I don't think it really made any difference except to soothe my guilty conscience. She didn't seem to realize that her two daughters were there.

Re the TV appearance: I received a letter out of the blue from Paul Rodriguez, a music publisher involved in the production, offering me the TV gig. After the concert, the guitarist (Bill) and I went for a drink with Paul. Bill was unhappy with his performance, and I didn't want him to say so in front of the publisher. Finally, at 2am, I was too tired to care and announced I was going to bed. Paul jumped up eagerly saying, "Me too!" I think he felt he'd done his duty by us! But a solid friendship between Paul and me was established; though little did I know then where this friendship would lead.

A few months later it seemed that Paul was ringing me rather a lot. He eventually explained that his marriage had broken up several months earlier and asked me out. We had a three-year courtship and married in August 1994. Paul had three children, one already a grown man with a house of his own; the second was a twelve-year-old girl, a sweetie and the apple of her father's eye, who chose to live with us; and the younger lad lived with us half the time. This is the best way to have children: older! No nappies, no all-night crying, and after the 'No' stage.

To be honest, I never really wanted children. I am the youngest child in my family and had absolutely no experience with them (being the one who was always babysat instead of babysitting). Also, when you teach as much as I did, it more than satisfies the maternal instinct. Actually, that's not an altogether true comment. I've been pregnant twice in my life, once for long enough for the hormones to kick in, making me want that baby – badly; the second time I didn't know I was pregnant until I aborted. I suppose I was getting a bit old by then to have a baby.

Anyway, I was very nervous about taking on a ready-made family. I'm happy to say that the nerves were unnecessary; we had a lot of fun. Lucy was at the age when you get embarrassed easily. It was hard not to take advantage of this! When we put her on the train to visit her grandmother, Paul and I would do a little dance on the platform. She would try to look like she didn't know us, but she had to peep out the window to see if we were still there.

I gave Lucy some flute lessons and sent her to Trinity College of Music Junior Department. Her musicianship was extraordinary, but the flute was not her instrument. She took up bassoon and was instantly enchanted. I rang up the Junior Department of the Royal Academy of Music and asked if they would like my stepdaughter as a pupil, and they offered a substantial scholarship. A month or so later, I rang them to say their bassoon teacher was not right for my daughter and they agreed to let her have lessons outside the school. Lucy was already sitting principal bassoon in the student orchestra.

However, Lucy chose to study anthropology at university, not music. She now works for her proud father and is herself one of the Directors of a small music publishing company.

In fact, all Paul's children take part in his business. The oldest child, Wayne, does the accounts. He went to university as a mature student and has a degree in business studies. But the real success story belongs to the youngest, Fred. Fred was born autistic and his parents were told to get used to the idea that he would be institutionalised. Fred's mother and father refused to accept this; they looked into music therapy, which apparently helped to some extent, and a new technique known as Holding Therapy – and now Fred is living and working in Burton-upon-Trent and is married to a lovely young lady. Fred, too, works for the family business via e-mail. In many ways, though the youngest, he is the only child who has 'left home'.

As I said, Paul and I were married in 1994. I am his third wife and I have told him to get used to me, because I'm here to stay!

Chapter 10 (Bob)

(1985 – 2008)

Lawrenceville is a town in Southside Virginia, about twenty miles north of the North Carolina border. African-Americans make up the great majority of residents, and in 1985 racial harmony lagged in comparison to the more urban areas of Virginia. As in many small southern towns, the United Methodist and the Baptist churches are the two largest in town. Accordingly, pastors are held in high esteem and are immediately welcomed with open arms. If they behave themselves and expend a serious effort in ministry, ministers of main line churches in more rural settings attain almost immediate 'Rock Star' status.

Martha John felt it would be best for her to stay at home and be a homemaker, mother and wife, rather than immediately seeking employment. She wisely never became involved in the church's organizational life or accepted a leadership role. She worshipped regularly, and every Sunday she and Elizabeth sat in the same pew inspiring me to be the best preacher I could be. For her role as the wife of this minister, I shall be eternally grateful. After our first year, Martha, with my urging, accepted a teaching position with the Brunswick County Public School System. Computer science was in its infancy in public education in the 1980s and Martha John set up the Computer Lab and Department, and taught higher mathematics in the high school.

We spent four years in this sleepy hamlet. My church work, as well as musical interests, flourished. The church was steeped in mid-twentieth century culture, a lag of some thirty years. Racial prejudice, even though this time frame embraced the final fifteen years of the twentieth century, was an unspoken fact of life. I became involved as an advisor and critic (for lack of a better term) to local courthouse politics. And I also became close friends with Tom Rylands, the Assistant Principal of the local junior high school. He is a good jazz clarinet and saxophone player, and in order to join Tom and others in the musical life of Lawrenceville, I dusted off my clarinet and the rest is a tale taller than I have space to write! This was to be my 'Jazz Period' as classical music was an unknown quantity in Southside Virginia.

A group of us organized a Dixieland Jazz Band, 'The Brunswick Stew', and we played regularly for about four years. This seeming diversion from my role as pastor was accepted with open arms by my Methodist parishioners. I suppose it gave the church a bit of notoriety it otherwise might not have gotten! Tom and his wife Ann became like family to Martha and me. The four of us spent a great deal of time together and enjoyed many joint vacations and other family events

The church was not a great challenge to me. Most of my ministerial effort was devoted to one-on-one as pastor and friend. The church neither grew nor lost members during our four-year stay in Lawrenceville. This was true despite the diminishing population of the area. Perhaps the ever-present economic hardship and the outdated racial divide in the community cast a pall on the citizenry that somehow kept the people, churches and institutions from achieving greater things.

Elizabeth grew into pre-adolescence while we were in Lawrenceville. Our once scrawny, spindly-legged seven-year-old began a rapid transformation into adolescence, before she officially became a teenager! Elizabeth at times resisted metamorphosis from little girl to womanhood; this resulted years later in her becoming a beautiful, successful and loving adult. Ashby, a six-pound Maltese puppy, became a member of our family and was to retain his position as family mascot for the next twelve years. And then, once again, the bishop called and we packed our meagre belongings and answered the call to the mountains of Virginia.

I was sent to, in consultation with the district superintendent and the bishop, the pulpit of St Johns United Methodist Church in Buena Vista, a small city nestled in a valley between the Blue Ridge and the Appalachian mountains in western Virginia. This was to be one of my more productive and memorable pastorates. But honesty compels me to admit that Martha's and Elizabeth's evaluations are not necessarily the same as mine.

In 1989, we arrived in what is one of the most beautiful areas of the State of Virginia. The mountains, as well as the quaintness of the culture, were an immediate source of happiness for us all. The church was a mid-sized, old structure that was most conducive to worship and reflection. It was in Buena Vista and St Johns that I broke the unwritten 'rule' of Methodism. The premise was that pastors stayed in one church no more than four years. I was to pastor this fine church for five years. The four-year rule was not a rule as much as a tradition. I can happily say that today this antiquated, unwritten tradition is dead and buried – as it should be!

When the church parsonage was built in 1927, it was a show place, a home any pastor family would be comfortable living in. In 1989 the parsonage was antiquated, suffering the consequences of poor maintenance and disrepair, and was generally a sub-standard residence. It was, quite honestly, the worse for wear as well as outmoded. I unsuccessfully petitioned the church to sell the house and purchase a new parsonage. The conservative element vetoed that idea. Rather than push the matter further and ruffle some feathers, Martha and I bought our own home on the side of a mountain, though still within the city limits. This was pretty much an unheard of thing for a parsonage family to do. The practice is accepted and encouraged today! For ten years we lived in our beloved mountain chalet. I dearly miss Martha, Elizabeth and our chalet – Ashby too!

During the entire time we were in Buena Vista, Martha John taught mathematics and science in one form or another in both the middle school and high school, as well as for a time in Stuarts Draft, some thirty-five miles away. Over the course of her teaching career, she excelled and 'raised the bar' in the area of teacher competence, and the art of educating and accepting the young as people of worth.

Though still a relatively young man, or so I thought, health issues were to crop up during this period. A herniated disc in my neck area resulted in cervical spinal surgery to alleviate excruciating pain, and a creeping numbness in my right arm. Surgery was completely successful, and to this day I have experienced no recurring symptoms. I was lucky that time! But little did I realize then that in the ensuing years, I would experience various and sundry physical deterioration that would threaten those activities I had grown to love.

We served on the American Red Cross local Chapter; I as the Disaster Chairperson, Martha the Blood Collection Chairperson. A major flood in Buena Vista in 1992 tested my ability as the one in charge of disaster relief. With God's help, as well as the hard-working cadre of volunteers in my area, the work was a success! Another responsibility I volunteered for was a seat on the Buena Vista Planning Commission. I served in this capacity for two years, and learned a great deal about my city and its people. But my entry into politics was short lived.

During this time, I was deepening my musical interests as well as in my chosen profession as a clergyman. I immediately fell into the company of the musicians of the area, and was immediately drafted into a recorder consort which opened up a whole new venue for me. At the same time, I organized a jazz quintet, 'Softouch'. We played extensively for civic events, political rallies, weddings, as well as dances and concerts. Quite often, Tom Rylands and Ann would come to Buena Vista when Softouch was playing and Tom would play with the band.

Quite by accident, I was to run across my high school sweetheart, Carolyn Ayers, who was a magnificent pianist and Head of the Organ Department of Hollins College in Roanoke, Virginia. We prepared a recital of recorder and piano music which was given in 1991 at St Johns Church to an overflow crowd of Early Music devotees or, perhaps – curiosity seekers. The following year, Carolyn and I gave a recital in the metropolitan Washington area for the Fine Arts Series of the Fairfax United Methodist Church. My musical diversions never detracted from my primary task of ministry to God's people. I would like to believe my music enhanced my work of the ministry.

During this period, I started teaching private trumpet and flute students in our home. As is quite often the case, only a few students are now fine instrumentalists in their own right. Of particular note is my prize trumpet student, Lisa Forman. She continues her studies with my dear friend, Dr John Brodie, the director of the V.M.I Regimental Band. Lisa now plays professionally in the western part of Virginia. She is in demand as a soloist in churches in the area. We talk on the phone on occasion and I am so proud of her accomplishments.

Two events that were among the most difficult I have ever been called on to do were officiating at the funerals of my close friends, Bob Hill and John Swisher. They, along with Tom Rylands, were as close as brothers to me. Also during our time in Buena Vista, Martha John and I were to lose our parents. These five years were a time of sadness as well as joy. The loss of our parents was a difficult thing – it still is. Her mother lingered for a couple of years in a local nursing facility. Martha's attention to her was an example of shear love and devotion.

St Johns Church grew during our five years there. Many of my dearest friends were elderly, as was the leadership of both the church and city. It was my lot to officiate at many a funeral of a close friend and mentor. Our time in Buena Vista and St Johns drew to an end in 1994 after five good, though at times difficult, years.

The Lord and the bishop, in their supposed wisdom, sent us to Portsmouth, Virginia, to West End United Methodist Church. This was a challenge to us as a family, and began a destructive process that would culminate in Martha and me getting divorced in 2001.

West End Church was composed of many of the finest lay-people it had been my privilege to serve. The geographic area was one of the least enjoyable I have ever lived in. We moved there in June of 1994. Elizabeth did not find the high school there bearable. She was constantly harassed, and taunted and abused by other students. In order to salvage her high school career and emotional health, we decided that she and Martha should move back to Buena Vista. In November they returned to the mountains, leaving me in Tidewater, Virginia. Once a week I travelled to Lawrenceville to play trumpet in a big band, see my friends and retain as much of my sanity as possible. As often as I could, I would travel to Buena Vista to see my family, and if need be, make simple repairs and perform maintenance on our mountain chalet and garden. One year in Portsmouth was the shortest pastorate in my career, and the low point of my ministry.

I told my district superintendent that I simply had to be moved in June to an appointment closer to Buena Vista and salvage, the best I could, our family. I was sent to Mt Tabor United Methodist Church as a reminder that I was not in charge of my fortunes. The bishop and his cabinet of some sixteen district superintendents made the decisions where a preacher was to be sent. My days in the Army seem to be the model for the Methodist Itinerant System – or, at least, it seemed so. Mt Tabor is a rural church near Harrisonburg, Virginia. Harrisonburg is a medium-size city, and the home of James Madison University, one of Virginia's state universities. Martha John and Elizabeth lived in Buena Vista where Elizabeth was putting the finishing touches on her high school education, and Martha taught at Parry McClure High School. All the while, I pastored my flock seventy miles to the north.

I would go home on Fridays and return Saturday evenings to conduct worship on Sunday morning. Martha John and Elizabeth were faithful in travelling the nearly seventy miles each way to be with me on Sundays. They would return home late on Sunday to our mountain chalet. Life during these years of separation and weekend reunions made an otherwise difficult life nearly impossible. Shared marital responsibilities often became individual responsibilities.

The church was diametrically opposed to my concept of the nature of the Church and Christian Theology. The musical fare was Southern Gospel, Blue Grass and, of course, Country Music. More importantly, these dear mountain folk had their ingrained ideas of theology and did not change any of them because a new preacher said they should. My frustration mounted, and our family life was strained by separation, financial problems, parenthood and my church work.

There was no open hostility evidenced between the membership and myself. I was too old to fight and the church people were also. I remained at Mt Tabor for two years and decided to retire at age sixty-two. It seemed like the only thing I could do to salvage what sanity I had left, and hopefully salvage what remained of Martha's and my marriage. So it was to be in June of 1997 I retired at the Virginia Annual Conference, walked across the stage, shook the bishop's hand, and along with the other forty or so retirees, received a cheap little plaque denoting some thirty-four years of faithful service to the Church.

I was a free man! Now I could move to my beloved Buena Vista mountain chalet and reap the fruits of my labours, all the while enjoying my family, my music and being 'my own person'. Utopia was right around the corner – or so I thought.

From June 1997 until June 1998, I enjoyed my new-found freedom, but missed the salary that was supplanted by a pension that paled in comparison. My private music teaching expanded. I had a studio in Covington, Virginia as well as in Buena Vista. During this time I avoided invitations to be a guest preacher and concentrated on my new-found secularization. There is an old saying that, 'Preachers never retire'. There may be a bit of truth in that as I began to miss the life of the church, as well as conducting worship and preaching. Martha found herself with more husband and less money to meet family financial needs.

In June of 1998, I accepted a part-time pulpit in a wonderful little church in the Shenandoah Valley. I served the Weyers Cave United Methodist Church for one year. Elizabeth became the Church Secretary during the summer for a pittance of a salary paid by me. I think she, to this day, believes the church paid her! Martha John, Elizabeth and I were together more than before I retired. On weekends she would drive the fifty miles from Buena Vista to attend church and mingle with the church folk. In every church we served, Martha John was beloved by the church members.

I had a cataract operation which, though routine, went awry. A few days after the operation, I was having serious pain in my left eye. On Easter Sunday of 2000, I fainted while preaching. Martha John immediately phoned the leading ophthalmologist in Roanoke and he was gracious enough to see me on Easter Sunday at his Eye Clinic. With rigorous treatment, subsequent operations for raging uveitis and vision threatening glaucoma, my sight was saved with a medium amount of permanent vision loss. After three operations, and inordinate amounts of eye drops, I will continue, till the last, paying the price for an incompetent and bungling eye surgeon in Lexington, Virginia. My regular visits to my ophthalmologist are, to this day, one of life's necessities!

My year at Weyers Cave Church as a part-time retired minister was both therapeutic and frustrating. The year kept me occupied with the church and private teaching. I would teach on Thursdays and Fridays, prepare for Sunday on Saturday, and take care of any pastoral work at the church on Monday and Tuesday. I visited my ophthalmologist every two weeks during most of this year. My vision was seriously impaired and it was necessary to enlarge sermons and scripture texts in order to read them from the pulpit.

It was during this time that I began noticing my thumbs were beginning to be painful. Everyday activities, like tying my shoes, buttoning a shirt, turning the page of Holy Writ – these and many other activities began to become a source of worry, and in a decade's time would necessitate my making painful decisions.

In October of 2000, after finishing my year at Weyers Cave Church, I, an otherwise deliberate preacher who seldom made decisions without weighing all possible outcomes, did the unthinkable. On a Friday morning, after Martha John had gone to school, I packed a few belongings and my musical instruments and left Buena Vista for good. In retrospect, I realize I was near, or on the verge of, some sort of mental or emotional collapse. For some time, financial problems and a lack of communication between Martha John and me had escalated rapidly. Neither of us was aware of the seriousness of our problems, or the consequences of unresolved and unarticulated differences in our marriage.

In the not too distant past our friends, Tom and Ann Rylands, had separated. I drove in a daze to Ann Rylands home in Lawrenceville. Familiar surroundings and a sympathetic listener drew me there. As time passed, Ann and I became more than friends and I moved in with her for the better part of a year. In time, it became apparent to both of us that we were not in love, just two very lonely and confused people who found solace in each other's company. Let me emphasize that Ann Rylands was not the reason or the cause of my leaving, and ultimately divorcing, Martha John. If a reason or motive is needed, all I can offer is extreme exhaustion, frustration and stupidity, all bordering on a nervous breakdown or emotional collapse.

During this time I taught at the Brunswick Academy, a prep school on the outskirts of Lawrenceville. I was employed to teach high school English as well as beginning a band. I confess that academically, as well as musically, I was totally out of my element. My apologies to the students who, for three years, suffered from my English teaching! I trust the instrumental students fared better.

My brother, Fred, visited me in Lawrenceville during Christmas of 2002. He suggested that I consider moving to Washington, North Carolina where he lived. Martha John and I had, a few years back, visited Fred in 'Little Washington', and I was impressed with the quaintness and friendliness of this area. The arrangement sounded good, we would add an addition onto the house he was buying to give us enough room to have the necessary space and solitude. In June of 2003, I moved in and have enjoyed every moment of my new-found home. I even purchased a Suzuki Bergman 650cc Scooter and am 'back in the saddle again'. My musical exploits are less ambitious than in the past, but nonetheless fulfilling.

Old age and over fifty years of playing the flute and clarinet (and maybe my motorcycling shares some of the blame) caused me to develop very painful arthritis in my thumbs, making playing the flute very difficult. I first noticed twinges of thumb pain in 1996, but it was so slight that I never gave it another thought until everyday tasks, such as tying ones shoes, buttoning buttons and eventually holding onto objects without dropping them, gave cause for alarm. In January of 2006, I had surgery on my right thumb. After many months of healing, the pain was gone except when I attempted to play the flute. Gone was any dexterity and ability to stretch my right hand.

These, as well as extreme pain playing the flute combined with a noticeable loss of finger technique and dexterity, brought on my retirement in 2006 from my beloved flute. I then found the trumpet could be managed without the hand and thumb pain. I have found reinventing myself as a trumpeter often comical as well as rewarding. It is said that, 'Idle Hands are the Devil's Workshop'. I found myself experimenting with playing the recorder again. Much to my surprise, the difference in hand position and finger motion between the traverse flute and the alto recorder enabled me to resurrect my recorder playing, and I am now able to perform on recorder as well as trumpet in public without embarrassing myself.

I cannot stop myself from making some brief but heart-felt comments or assessments of the United Methodist Church in America, as seen by a retired pastor looking back on the past forty-four years as an ordained Elder in the Virginia Conference of the United Methodist Church. There is a very brief text in Holy Writ that goes something like this, 'Jesus wept.' He was not weeping for Himself, but for his beloved Jerusalem. I weep not for myself, but for my beloved Church that has seemingly lost its way. The faithful, struggling church where the gospel was unashamedly preached has given way to the Mega Church as the modern Body of Christ.

As a minister, I never operated as one who represented a gigantic corporation or a small business. I was, for lack of a better term, a pastor – a shepherd to the people God entrusted to my keeping. In addition to winning new souls to the family of God, I was a shepherd.

Certainly there were those United Methodist pronouncements and quadrennial programmes I considered perversions of the mission of the Church. There were those preachers, TV evangelists, charlatans, faith healers and soothsayers, as well as aspiring bishops, who obviously were in it for the power, prestige or the money. There were then, and there are today, those who will seek to promote self above all else, and will do so until God brings down the curtain on the drama of life.

My heartache has been directed at the United Methodist churches, ministers, superintendents and bishops who saw the answer to steadily diminishing church rolls to be – *entertainment.* Give the people a good time; preach that God wants for them to be rich and happy. I know of a United Methodist church that is modelled after a circus – replete with tigers, elephants and other circus animals. It is said that a popcorn machine is located in that church's sanctuary, or midway, whichever best fits.

The Church has historically had, as its handmaiden, great music. The great composers were often church musicians, Kappel Meisters or Directors of Music Ministries as we often refer to them today. The Church, throughout its history, with rare exceptions, paid its musicians a paltry salary, but at least many a fine musician found within the Church a home, a place to compose, direct, perform – all for the glory of God.

Sadly, many United Methodist churches have taken a cue from the entertainment world. Instead of the great music of yesterday, as well as today, we are subjected to either 1970s Coffee House style 'Christian Gospel' (which is neither Christian nor gospel) or pseudo rock and roll versions of a 'be happy and feel good' religion.

The beautiful gothic or classic sanctuaries have given way to Multimedia or Multi-purpose rooms with large screens for the words of the songs, thus negating the need for hymnals. Hymnals are often being replaced with little paper-bound gospel songbooks. Sorry about that Charles Wesley, old chap!

Rick Warren (a young minister of a 30,000 member Mega Church whose message is God wants you to be happy, wealthy and give his church all your money – a real opportunist and purveyor of a 'feel good, touchy feely religion') is a prime example; dress casually – like you are going to a baseball game instead of the pulpit to lead in worship. Gone are clergy in dark suits, robes, or vestments of any sort. Symbolism is rapidly becoming a relic of the past, largely because many people under fifty were not reared in the church and find religious symbolism too mystical.

Many denominations other than the Southern Baptists (who never used symbolism to any extent) are offering two services on Sunday: a 'contemporary' service and a 'traditional' service. The contemporary services are into popular music; the lyrics are a watered down, incomplete version of the Gospel Message. The music is a trite conglomeration of country music, rock and southern gospel in a sort of folk music setting. A *Kum Ba Ja*, sit around the camp fire idea.

I realize, sadly, that so much of the decline in the worship experience is a direct result of the churches being filled with 'spiritual pygmies' whose acquaintance with the Church came rather late in life.

I conclude this homily with a biblical mandate that is to 'Worship the Lord in Spirit and in Truth'. I submit that in this Post-Christian era we are consciously and intentionally avoiding both.

Chapter 11 (Ann)

(1999 – 2008)

If my memory is right – I lied about my age for so long that dates are vague! – it was in 1999 that I joined the ABRSM (Associated Board of the Royal Schools of Music) as a Mentor on their Certificate of Teaching course. When I went on the three-day training session, I noticed my right hand was shaking. I attributed this to exhaustion and nerves, but the tremor continued after I returned home.

From that point, it seems as if everything happened at once.

One day I was walking down a fairly steep staircase at Trinity when suddenly the most excruciating pain shot through my ankle. I thought I had broken a bone, but my GP sent me to the hospital for tests and it proved to be arthritis. I was encouraged to have an arthroscopy immediately. In and out the same day, I was told, and only a local anaesthetic. In fact, I was kept in hospital for three days and given a general anaesthetic, which made me feel quite ill. I think that the arthroscopy triggered the approaching Parkinson's disease. I had agreed to play in a little concert two days after the hospital released me. I should have cancelled, but at the time I felt I could manage. I was totally unprepared for my lack of breath control. I am quite small, so my breath control has always, of necessity, been good. Not so on that occasion!

Another time I was invited to give a recital for a music society in Portsmouth and once again my breath control was suddenly missing. This was an important concert and I was playing with a brilliant guitarist, Roland Gallery, music that I love. Once again I was embarrassed by an inability to maintain decent breath control.

Then one day I noticed that one of my fingers was bending in the wrong direction, making flute playing impossible. I used a rubber band as a sort of splint to keep my finger over the key, but that only worked for a little while. In the middle of a recording session I had to send in a replacement. My flute-playing days were ended.

Yet another disturbing factor was that I lost a lot of weight – a stone and a half, and in a fairly short space of time – and I was never a fat person. My GP tested me for diabetes and other ailments. I can't remember them all now, but I think we both knew all along what the trouble really was. Finally he sent me to a neurologist.

I was devastated when my unspoken fears of Parkinson's disease were confirmed. It felt like a death sentence. No, it was worse – a death sentence is finite. PD does not kill, it gradually destroys the body. My poor husband was going to watch me deteriorate over the years, becoming an ever-growing burden on him.

My sister had a friend who worked at the Mayo Clinic, and she did a little research and located a well-respected neurologist in London who agreed to put me on his list of patients. The neurologist was able to determine that I had been showing signs of PD for the three preceding years (since 1997), and started me on Amantadine; but Amantadine left me totally disorientated, so he switched me to Sinemet and told me to go back in four months. The only guidance I received was to build up the dosage gradually and not to take more than five tablets a day. I didn't know what to expect or what to watch out for, and I can look back now and see that I was overdosing, hence the cramping and jerking in my legs.

When I left Trinity after twenty-eight years of teaching there, my husband Paul arranged a bang-up retirement present for me: a trip to the States to visit my family members and see where they lived, as well as taking in the West Coast. (The touring orchestra I played with while I was still living in America covered a few thousand miles, but we never got west of Kansas and South Dakota.) Paul and I visited my sister in Wisconsin, my cousin in Oklahoma and my brother in South Carolina, finally spending a few days in California. I hadn't seen my brother, Mike, for several years and I don't know how to begin to describe the emotional impact of that visit. He was (he's no longer living) a recovered alcoholic but he was also a genius – he went off all the IQ tests when he was in school, his paintings are hanging in museums and he wrote a novel titled *On High Steel* which was a bestseller. Mike was bored to tears in a small town with no intellectual stimulus. Paul, with his usual insight, said, "Let's buy him a computer." We had one delivered to him and before long, Mike was building the damn things himself!

But eventually we had to return to real life. Paul had a business to run. I went to bed. For a *very* long time. No longer could I hide from the fact that I have Parkinson's disease, and I was depressed. I couldn't hold a flute any more – my fingers wouldn't function as they should. Playing and teaching were all I knew. I'm ashamed to admit it, but I wallowed in self-pity. Finally one day I said to my husband, "I'm bored."

He replied, "Why don't you write that novel you've been talking about for years?" (That insight of his again, recognizing exactly what would pull me out of the doldrums!) So I did – and it was published, disproving the not-so-wise saying that 'You can't teach an old dog new tricks.' I also joined a poetry workshop, one of the most fulfilling things I've ever tried.

I also resolved not to become a victim of this insidious disease.

The American Parkinson's Disease Society runs an on-line forum where you can write in with questions, and read the answers to everyone's queries. I read it avidly and soon discovered that (1) PD medications mask the disease, they don't cure it, and (2) all PD medications can have side effects, no matter what the neurologist tells you, and (3) a neurologist's skill comes into being when he starts balancing one drug against another. It's horrendous the number of drugs that people with advanced PD play off against each other! I vowed to myself that I would find a way to delay that stage as long as possible. It also seemed to me that I should take responsibility for my own health and not rely on doctors, no matter how eminent they may be. Don't get me wrong – I think doctors, certainly the ones I've had, are wonderful. But there are a lot of unknowns in PD and it makes me happy to think that maybe an optimistic approach helps, and that my own small efforts to slow the progression down have done some good. And I have the security of knowing that the neurologist is there if I need him.

Regarding my left hand, the middle finger bends over to the left and it is nearly impossible to bring it back. My GP sent me to a hand specialist who sent me to a splint specialist who devised a contraption that covered all of my hand. When I was eventually allowed to remove it, my whole hand was stiff. The hand specialist then said I should never have had that type of splint; it's a shame he didn't monitor my case and tell me sooner! I was then sent to an orthopaedic surgeon and then to a plastic surgeon, and then to a rheumatologist; after three years I ended up with the splint specialist again. The last time I saw her, this lady said she would write to me with a follow-up appointment; that finally happened a whole year later.

A nurse told me that in my hospital notes my finger is described as 'pseudo-rheumatoid'. My guess is that I was, at this juncture, in the early stages of rheumatoid arthritis, even though it didn't show up in my blood tests. Apparently this is fairly often the case.

On the off chance that Parkinson's was responsible for my distorted hands, I contacted the helpline of the American PD Society about my fingers. They said they have never heard of this problem connected with PD and suggested I visit a rheumatologist. (I didn't tell them I had already done so.) My regular neurologist said he had often seen this problem and it is definitely connected with PD.

I think there is a great danger, when you have a disorder like Parkinson's disease, of blaming it for all your aches and pains.

A friend said to me, "Why don't you visit my kinesiologist?" I didn't know what a kinesiologist was. I'm not sure I do even now! But when I first went to see this man, I was having difficulty swallowing and my skin, especially on my forehead, was rough and sore and unsightly. When I had asked a neurologist (a stand-in for my regular one) about my skin, he replied, "I don't know anything about that. I'm not a dermatologist." It seemed an odd answer, since skin problems are one of the symptoms/side effects of PD – and neurologists work with drugs that treat the symptoms, not the disease itself. As yet there is no drug that cures Parkinson's disease.

Kinesiology is a natural health therapy which uses muscle-testing procedures to help the kinesiologist 'read' your body. It's rather like acupuncture but using the muscles instead of the nerves. When I first went to my friend's practitioner, I was almost overwhelmed with the strangeness of this technique (you hold your arm out while he uses the arm rather like a lever) and I thought to myself, 'What have I got myself into?'

By the way, the kinesiologist I see would probably not call himself a skin specialist either; but he worked with me and now my skin is much improved, and I only have swallowing difficulties when I'm tense. Difficulty with swallowing is usually a later stage problem. This is one of the difficulties with Parkinson's: it advances at different speeds and in different ways with everybody.

Other things which were bothering me when I first went to see Tim (the kinesiologist) included an inability to tie my shoelaces or handle a knife and fork comfortably (though I suspect some of my difficulties were aggravated by the arthritis – in spite of the fact that the doctors couldn't agree at that time that I was arthritic!). Doing up buttons was also a monumental feat. Now I have considerably less hassle with buttons, laces or cutlery (I couldn't carve a roast, however!). Yet, I'm on the same medication I was put on several years ago (Sinemet, three times a day, and Selegiline). In other words, Tim is treating the symptoms at least as well as, if not better than, a neurologist could. And he is doing it without using drugs with side effects.

One of the symptoms which I am now experiencing, and that apparently can't be treated with PD drugs or natural therapies, is loss of balance. According to my neurologist, the only thing that might possibly – not definitely – help is Amantadine. And I can't take that. Plus, the side effects of Amantadine for a person in their mid-sixties include hallucinations. That frightens me. Not long ago, I met a woman also suffering from PD who said to me, "I see things that I know aren't there and yet they are there. It's frightening." I haven't seen her since.

I am also seeing regularly a friend of Tim's, a hypnotherapist. George has helped me to put on some weight. I had got down to six stone (that's eighty-four pounds) and that in itself was enough to make me vulnerable in crowds. George also keeps my spirits up. But he is doing much more than this. He is carrying out research on how the mind can be used to heal the body.

Parkinson's disease is caused by a degeneration of the brain cells which produce dopamine. Dopamine affects our movements, our emotional responses and also the ability to feel pain and pleasure. I read somewhere that by the time PD is diagnosed, the majority of those cells have died.

Actually, experiments with stem cell research are producing exciting results and it probably won't be long before curative measures are found for several horrific diseases such as Parkinson's and Alzheimer's. But, until a cure is found, I feel I have been one of the lucky sufferers thanks to friends like Tim and George and – most important of all – my husband, Paul.

Food for Thought

Why do some people suffer a malady like arthritis or Parkinson's disease and others not? Bob and I set out to try to unravel this mystery by writing about our lives in detail. He now feels he can relate, at least to some extent, his arthritis to riding a motorcycle for years without the aid of heated hand controls or heated gloves. I can relate to this too! He also feels lack of proper practice techniques damaged his fingers. Again, me too. Relating Parkinson's disease to a head injury when I was six years old is trickier; but when you add to this a further head injury when I was in my early twenties, it perhaps becomes more plausible. One thing, however, that we both have realized, is that life is precious. Having an incurable disease does not mean you can't do anything at all. It means you have to find other things to do.

When my parents first retired, Daddy and Mother busied themselves by going to concerts and participating in amateur ensembles. But as they became less mobile, they became more and more bored and depressed. My father said to me one day, "I hope you never have to play solitaire. It's all I have to do." It was heartbreaking! He had thought that when he retired he would devote more time to composition – write a second string quartet and other goodies (his first string quartet won a national competition); but he had no piano.

"The house is too small," said Mother, when I offered to rent one for them. And it's true, the house *was* small. But they could have put a little upright in one of the bedrooms.

The trouble is, problems which seem to be unsolvable at the time often are simple in hindsight.

Certainly Mother was in a deep depression, but she did make an effort to interest her husband in a hobby. One pastime she encouraged was making tapestries. Well, good for her; at least she tried to interest him in something. I think, however, somewhere inside he felt humiliated and useless.

When Charles, one of my father's former pupils, visited England, Mother wouldn't let him see Daddy. She didn't want anyone to see her witty professor in his current state of health. She wanted his friends and pupils to remember him as he had been. I will always wonder if that was a mistake; the visit might have done Daddy some good.

I also can't help but wonder if my Dad's Alzheimer's would have progressed more slowly had he been able to compose. I know boredom was killing both my parents. I believe that keeping busy is absolutely essential, both for mental and for physical health. But no one who hasn't been there understands how hard it is to keep busy when you are tired all the time. Sometimes life sucks, doesn't it?

You know what I hate the most? Seeing the pity in a friend's eyes. A close friend of many years standing invited my husband and me out to lunch. It was one of those days when the shaking was bad, and my friend was unable to keep the sorrow he felt, hidden. I do not want to be pitied.

Mind the Gap
(sharing some relevant emails)

(Closing Doors)   (8 December 2006)

Dear Bob

I know things have to change in this world, but it's sad that RPI doesn't exist anymore. I taught at two conservatories in London. Largely because of financial problems, the London College of Music had to merge with a university and has now virtually disappeared. While it was artistically bottom of the five music schools then in London (in the '70s and '80s) nevertheless some of my best pupils were LCM students. Being bottom in London is still above most of the rest of the country! I was Head of Woodwind there and I accepted, occasionally, students with talent who needed remedial technical work. Mostly it was a successful approach – my woodwind teachers were tops! However, most of my teaching was at Trinity College of Music, a very good music school where students with severe technical problems weren't often accepted. Trinity, too, suffered financial difficulties and had to vacate their premises in the centre of London. Trinity managed to get a beautiful building in South London – but the kudos of the central London location was gone, and I think that has given the college a hurdle or two to overcome.

I took early retirement just before the move. I'm grateful to have been there during Trinity's heyday.

(The Rest of the Story)   *(9 December 2006)*

Dear Bob

You ask about the TV recital I did. There's a whole story behind that performance. Mother was ill – very ill – and I was afraid I would have to cancel the performance. An opportunity like that comes only once in a lifetime and if I cancelled, I wouldn't get another chance. My sister dropped everything and flew over to be with Mother, leaving me free to do the concert. As if that weren't trouble enough, the guitarist (Bill) and the harpist (Heulwen) hated each other. Each was complaining to me separately about the other. They only got on the concert because of me! I was determined to make the most of the opportunity; I gave up a lot for it – not being with Mother when she needed me.

As it happens, Mother didn't die for another day. I like to think she waited for my return.

Another concert was filmed before mine which seemed to take a lot of time, so I didn't play until about midnight. The audience had to stay awake – they were brought in especially for the evening. Because it was so late, I felt we couldn't ask for a replay of anything. After all, you don't get a replay in a live concert! But that's why an opening guitar chord in the Handel is missing.

Also, that was how I met Paul. He was co-ordinating the music (getting copyright matters solved, etc). Someone had put my name forward (I never found out who) and it was Paul who wrote the letter offering me the gig.

Bill liked the Handel sonatas at a slower speed than I did, so I used to do a lot of ornaments to pass the time!

(Learning Humility)   *(13 December 2006)*

Dear Bob

Last night my PD support group had their annual Christmas party. The entertainment was one man (Indian) who brought a pre-recorded rock band on tape, while he sang and played guitar – largely '60s and '70s music. Trouble was, he didn't tune his guitar to the backing tracks. My initial reaction (when I could pull myself away from focusing on the foul intonation!) was, isn't this a stupid form of entertainment for a room full of people who can hardly walk? But several people got up to dance. One woman got out of her wheelchair and used it as a prop to lean on, while she moved her legs and wiggled her hips. Another man was standing, hardly able to move at all, and it wrenched my heart watching him – until I realised he had a big grin on his face and was enjoying himself immensely. I felt humbled. I learned an important lesson last night, but it's hard to put it into words. I hope I will never again underestimate disabled people. Small pleasures give great satisfaction. It was nice of the committee to arrange a Christmas party that made everyone feel normal. And wonderful of them to create an atmosphere where no one felt embarrassed by their disabilities.

(Confession is Good for the Soul)   *(16 December 2006)*

Dear Ann

Now I have a confession to make. Have you ever done something, behaved in a manner that you were sorry for? Well, I was bad at our choir rehearsal this morning – the Christmas Cantata Dress Rehearsal.

There is an old man that I really try to avoid, but as luck will have it – we stood next to each other in the loft. He can't read well, sings out of tune and had the unmitigated gall to say out loud that I was singing a section wrong. Now, I have been known to sing wrong notes – but in tune! The church was cold, I was shaking from the cold and this old geezer 'plucked my nerve' with his constant jabs. Your father had a term for people like him who dabble in music – dilettante. Milton liked that word and applied it freely!

Thanks for letting me blow off steam – like you had any choice!

(Getting the Melody Right)   *(17 December 2006)*

Dear Bob

That old man sounds like bad news. I can't imagine you other than charming, and I have no doubt you always sing the right notes! That reminds me of when I was at the Cleveland Institute of Music; my best friend was a harpist and I can't imagine how she got into a reasonably good music conservatory. She sang everything wrong, with no idea that she was other than right. I used to stand beside her in the choir and the conductor (a dirty old man! But that's another story) apparently thought the weird notes were coming from me. I started arriving for choir rehearsal at the last minute to avoid standing by her.

(On Snow Cats)   (27 January 2007)

Dear Bob

We actually had SNOW a couple of days ago. It stayed around all morning but was totally gone by afternoon. Reminds me of a snowfall we had here in 1976. I had a cat who had been kept inside because I lived on a main road; that year I bought a little house with a teensy garden and Percy (the cat) was able to go outside. It was the first snow he had seen. At first he was tentative, sticking out a paw and hastily pulling it back. But a very short while later, I looked out and he was taking a running start and then sliding the length of the garden. It was obviously a great game!

Percy was a very special cat. Once I gave him a bath to get rid of fleas, and although cats aren't supposed to like water, Percy apparently liked getting rid of the fleas. After that, whenever I filled the bathtub, we used to have a race to see which of us got to it first! He lived to be seventeen, not a bad age for a cat.

(On worsening conditions)   *(21 March 2007)*

Dear Bob

I went to my PD support group meeting last night and was distressed to see that one of the members – he came to my summer party – had deteriorated to such an extent that he could hardly move. All this deterioration within a month. Horrid, insidious disease!

My PD specialist is fed up with me because I won't take the medication he wants to give me. Anyway, he is leaving working for the National Health and is going private, so I will be shifted to someone else. The disease is worsening – but slowly, so I won't complain.

(Of Queens and Thumbs)   *(4 May 2007)*

Dear Ann

Well, your Queen is over here in the US. She visited William and Mary College in Williamsburg, Friday. My daughter is a faculty member there and they have been doing a lot in recent weeks to make Queen Elizabeth's visit a memorable one. She was here fifty years ago, but I doubt if she comes in another fifty. One never knows!

You asked about my thumb(s). Since you asked, here is a brief description of my visit, Thursday, to the orthopaedic surgeon who did the operation.

When he asked me how my hand was, I said, "It hurts as much as it did before the operation, but now I have hardly any motion in the thumb. Playing the flute – the reason I had the operation – is still painful and I cannot play the little finger keys of the right hand."

He hummed and hawed, and said, "Come back in a couple months. It should be much better."

So, life goes on and I will give the flute another test run in a few weeks. In the meantime, the weather has turned cold (again) and very windy. As happens here, spring lasts one or two days and then – summer arrives and it will be 95 degrees!

I am not complaining!

(Recorder Delivery)   (13 May 2007)

Dear Ann

I did a funny thing today at church. I neglected to tell you that while the alto recorder is worse on my thumbs than the flute, the smaller soprano, or descant, due to its size, is easier to manipulate and gives no pain of any consequence.

This diatribe is background to my playing the soprano recorder with the anthem today. It went really well… recorder is so easy to blow, tone etc are all a matter of conceptualisation – if you know how you want it to sound, you can do it! Finger technique is a real BEAR!! The piece was real easy – my kind of piece.

A funny tale about the descant recorder and me: I gave up alto recorder in 1992, as well as clarinet, because they both were causing the thumb problem to worsen. The descant, because of its size, requires no stretch of the hands. Honestly, it doesn't hurt. I tried the alto last week, and it HURT!

Back to my story: I owned a Moeck Ebony wood Descant which I paid $230 for in 1981. I played descant seldom as the alto is the solo recorder. I played very little consort music. In 1990 I was asked to play the Sammartini *Concerto* in F Major with the Roanoke Virginia Symphony. I jumped at the chance, went to the first rehearsal and the fine, Ebony recorder played terribly. I switched to a $4.50 plastic Dolmetsch (English made) descant, it was wonderful. I played the performance on the little plastic recorder. I would never part with that instrument!

(Reflecting on Flutes)   *(25 May 2007)*

Dear Bob

Did I ever tell you the story of the Christmas I wasn't given a flute? When I was in my early teens, I wanted a flute for Christmas (I was using a school instrument). My special present that year was the same shape and weight as a flute, and I was sure that's what it was. I boasted to my parents that I knew what was in that box. Well, I was wrong. It was a silver-plated brush and mirror set. I had to pretend I had guessed correctly so as not to upset my parents, but when I was able to, I shut myself in my bedroom and cried. I was given a flute for my next birthday, by which I have to conclude that I didn't manage to hide my disappointment very well.

(Changing Standards)   *(21 June 2007)*

Dear Bob

The values of life change as we get older and what once seemed so important, now takes a lower position in our lives – sometimes this way of thinking is forced upon us! But I'm a great believer in the adage, 'When one door closes, another opens.' Sometimes opening that new door is difficult! Especially if one (like you and me) has put everything into one basket. If I were to tell you that writing poems takes the place of performing music in my life, I would be lying. The composing helps, but it's not the same. I never really studied composition and it is unlikely I will publish anything I'm writing. But it doesn't matter. What does matter (to me, anyway) is that I make the greatest effort I can, not to be a burden on others as my physical body gives out. And while I'm at it, to learn to appreciate the many wonderful things that exist on this earth. If this is the finale of my life, let it have many themes! (Pretty corny, huh?)

(Top Brass)   (26 June 2007)

Dear Ann

I am fine, just had a spurt of activity! Music jobs are increasing – trumpet and an occasional flute gig which is fine. After thirty minutes playing flute, it gets painful. Trumpet doesn't hurt anything but the hearer's ears!

Since you are worried about me, dear girl, I must confess I am worried about you too. Please tell me if your legs still hurt as much as they did a week or so ago. The only ailments I have are not life threatening… just life dulling. Aside from bad eyes (glaucoma), ringing in the ears (from years of flute playing), messed up thumbs and a BIG tummy – I am almost fine!

(Mob Rule)   (7 July 2007)

Dear Bob

I had a session with the hypnotherapist this morning and had to brave the underground. Bombs don't scare me. Crowds do.

The alternative treatments I am following through seem to be doing some good. The kinesiologist fights my PD with healthier tablets – mostly, I think, dietary supplements – rather than the chemicals the neurologists work with, although it is rather expensive. I get the chemical drugs for free; I have to pay (lots) for the 'natural' pills. And the hypnotherapist keeps my spirits up, heightens my appetite and helps me find the energy to do things, like write poems and music.

(Fiddling in the Wind)   (28 July 2007)

Dear Ann

My musical life has been fiddling around with various instruments, but each individually and for relative lengthy periods of time, instead of really mastering one. I have had love affairs with trumpet, clarinet, saxophone and flute. Each had its moments, each was loved (still is) by your aging accomplice.

The only thing ever dealt me that I could not beg, buy, lie or steal my way out of are these wretched thumbs! I confess they have stumped me. The problem started many years ago with the clarinet and the recorder. I spent inordinate amounts of time, though in widely different years, practising them. In 1994, it became apparent to me that the clarinet had to go. I wasn't very upset as the clarinet had been my protagonist for so many years.

Since the flute started out simply as a recreational activity, I grew to love the flute because I have a great affinity for recreation! I suppose I never sweat blood over the flute, every minute I played it was a joy. So, after fifty years of on-off again playing (mostly on), it is a loss that I will have to live with.

Lord, what a dissertation this has become. It is therapeutic for me to assemble my thoughts and write this wandering account of my musical life. And, of course, my inquiring mind drew me, over the years, to conducting and composition.

I really think, beyond any shadow of a doubt, that you did it the right and sensible way. You started with the flute and stayed with the flute.

(Bound and Rebound)   (31 August 2007)

Dear Ann

About the years 1976–1985: this nine-year chunk of my life was stressful, busy, wicked, spiritual, as well as chock full of new musical adventures, all interspersed with my divorce from Ann. She and I have two grown children, both of whom we are very proud. Ann and I have managed to maintain a good relationship; we both recognize the benefit this has for the children and our three grandchildren.

Ann is a pianist with an enormous personality that lights up a dark room. In fact everyone loves her, she is so extroverted and insane. To all appearances we were happy, but in fact we went our separate ways and saw each other at dinner (usually taken at a restaurant).

One December evening, I was watching television, December 3, 1984 it was – I will never forget it! Ann walked into the room and announced she was leaving me. I was shocked and hurt. "Don't let the door hit you in the butt on the way out," I growled.

I am guilty of making the biggest, dumbest mistake one can make. Counsellors, ministers (I am one), psychologists, drunken friends and total strangers will advise you not to marry on the rebound. But I did just that. In October 1985 – the 6th (my birthday) – I recited the solemn vows of holy matrimony to a truly lovely lady, some thirteen years my junior. Martha John Blair became Martha John Hawkins for the next fifteen years. She had a six-year-old daughter from her previous marriage. Her first husband had also been a Methodist minister. A touch of déjà vu here perhaps?

I left Martha in 1991. This is probably the biggest mistake I ever made, for Martha John is a brilliant, loving, giving, esoteric soul. If we could have had more time together, alone, I am sure we would be married to this day.

Time has passed, and any regrets I may have had are dissipated to the point that they are invisible.

In 1981, I accepted the pulpit (kitchen and the entire kettle of fish) of Pace Memorial Methodist Church in Richmond. As it was on the V.C.U. Campus, a part of my assignment was being minister to some twenty-five thousand university students. I also had a regular church in Pace Memorial. Due to location (ghetto), across the street from Monroe Park (the sight of numerous murders and stabbings), I conducted my ministry amongst the old Richmond dowagers and millionaires, as well as a goodly number of street people, homeless and some trying to stay drunk to avoid realizing what a mess they had made of their lives.

I did this for three or so years. If I wasn't schizophrenic at birth, I might become one in this unique situation. To balance my time with the disinherited children of God, I spent time at the music school, played the recorder like there was no tomorrow, and gave all sorts of socially correct recitals at the artistically accepted Richmond venues.

One such of these Early Music Groups was comprised of three neurotic, pre-menopausal women: a cellist, a harpsichordist and a player on the Baroque flute. I held down the recorder responsibilities. The group was called the 'James River Waites'. There was some old-world significance to that somehow, but I never really connected it to us. The group played rather well, but all of my jazz and symphony friends were merciless in the teasing: 'Bob and His Harem of Rejects', or something silly like that.

The ministerial responsibilities were immense. The 1980s was a period of an influx of homeless people from the north. The majority were addicted to drugs, whiskey or, as were some I caught, drinking shaving lotion. Much of my time was spent trying to keep them from freezing to death in the winter or getting knifed or mugged in the park across from my church. Quite a few of these dear souls were mentally not well.

Much Love, Bob

PS: I believe we humans can will ourselves sick and can will ourselves well. I believe in positive use of self-hypnosis, and can pretty much control my blood pressure, pulse and reaction to pain, somewhat.

I guess growing up in a minister's family and then spending nearly forty years as a minister steered me in the path of orthodoxy. My religious faith is a form of neo-orthodoxy, tinged with a little radical theology and the Social Gospel.

Faith healing is an interesting topic.

(Speaking with the Dead)   (14 September 2007)

Dear Bob

I used to have all of Edgar Cayce's books, but I think most of them have disappeared over the years. I limited what I said about the College of Psychic Studies for fear you would think I'm some kind of weirdo. But since you ask, I will elaborate somewhat.

Off and on, I visited Spiritualist churches where the guest medium gives messages to some of the visitors (congregation). Have you ever visited a Spiritualist church? Sometimes the medium is right, sometimes s/he is obviously missing the mark. But I went one evening to a church where the guest medium was Geoff Boltwood. He was breathtaking! He brought me a man, he said, carrying a violin (this was shortly after Daddy died). He talked on and on about Daddy and I am sorry to say, I can't remember most of it now. But Geoff was spot on. At the end of the 'service', I went up to him to say thanks for the message, and he gave me his card. I ended up taking some private lessons with him in mediumship.

While I'm on the subject of parents and other worldly communication, I will tell you another strange story. You know, I suppose, that Mother was a smoker (so was Daddy, but he quit when they came to England). After Mother died, I caught the train to Burghfield Common to arrange for the sale of their house contents. It was a tearful day. I waited for the return train to London feeling depressed. When the train pulled up to the platform, I couldn't get on the nearest carriage because of the strong smell of cigarette smoke. I got on the next car clearly marked 'No smoking'. When the train pulled into the London station, I looked at the car I had avoided and it, too, was a no smoking carriage. I reckon

Mother was there with me and identified herself through the cigarette smoke.

I was also attending the College of Psychic Studies, taking one to two day workshops as well as a class or two. Arthur Molinary was particularly interesting. He has worked with the police. His class was mediumship and I managed to get a couple of things right, but I was never really good at it. The class was really intended for advanced students, of which I was not one.

I took a class with Robin, a psychic who was teaching us how to use relaxation to further psychic development. One evening, he decided to try us on a kind of clairaudience. Robin went around the room trying to get each of us to let someone speak through us. I was dreading it as he got closer and closer to me, and when he asked me to speak up, I thought to myself, 'I can't do this.' Robin insisted I open my mouth and say something, anything. I did and suddenly I was jabbering away as a sailor named Jack. Now you probably think I'm delusional! I talked about how I had sailed around the world when I was alive and now I was sailing the seven seas of life (okay, I was corny). But there was a very strange feeling in my throat, and I had the impression the whole time that he had a hand on my shoulder.

I also took a healing course, but it wasn't my calling either.

I took some classes with Keith Casburn, both in the college and in his home, where he occasionally held workshops. Keith was such a good person that he almost glowed, and his classes were always warm and friendly. I felt honoured that he let me attend his home workshops as they were much sought after, and the space in his house was small-ish. His classes at the college were always well attended.

You say you believe we humans can will ourselves sick and can will ourselves well. This is what the hypnotherapist is trying to prove with me. And although it's not accepted by orthodox medicine, I think it's working.

Now, Bob, I hope I have not worried you.

Much love, Ann

(On saving and saviours)   *(15 September 2007)*

Dear Ann

Your last email was really special! I read with a great deal of interest your discussion of the spiritual aspects of healing. To put it in perspective from my point of reference, I strongly believe in the presence of faith healing as well as the human ability to, through the power of the mind and spirit, reach out to the 'spirit world'. Psychic phenomena and orthodox Christianity are not too far apart. Mostly, the differences come about from road blocks imposed by semantics, as well as definitions of spiritual things that may be a bit limited.

I understand that there were writings included in early biblical translations that no longer are a part of Holy Writ, because they were removed from time to time by overly zealous councils and individuals in the Early Church (100–400AD and perhaps beyond).

My path has been more than satisfactory to me; some of the differences in my Christian belief system and yours are really insignificant – just a matter of assigned labels and definitions. So, whether you believe it or not, the following assessment of your spiritual good health is predicated on my knowledge of a very lovely and talented young lady.

Do I believe you are 'saved' in the stodgy orthodox definition of salvation and all it entails? Certainly! Will you ascend the stairway to heaven and stand at the pearly gates, and try to convince St Peter that you need a Powell, not a Haynes Conservatory flute, for eternity? Yes I do. Even if you have to play a standard sterling, handmade, soldered tone-hole model without a 14kt lip plate. Those extravagances are reserved for the saints – you nor I fit into that stodgy category, I fear!

If you ever speak to me again after this email, I will be lucky. Remember, Ann, in spite of how high your blood pressure goes while reading this, just remember you are more important to me than I want to admit.

On what basis do I so boldly involve myself in your spiritual journey? What right do I have? Well, you brought it up! Now, do I really, honestly believe in eternal life? Yep! Do I believe that you and I shall, one fine day, with young bodies, agile thumbs and you with not a pain in the world (or for that matter, out of the world), just as steady as the Rock of Gibraltar – that we shall play flute duets and enjoy all those things we may not have had the opportunity to experience in this life.

Why do I say you are saved? By the way, I detest that term, or at least the connotation it conjures up, due to misuse over the centuries. I can tell in my heart – soul – psychic hat that you are a person of great love for humanity, things of beauty as so obvious in your quest for the lovely. Your flute playing was a spiritual experience for so many, many people. The flute was taken from you, by an evil force (disease). You responded through writing music, prose and poetry. Your quest for the beautiful (spiritual) would not 'roll over and play dead'.

To me, and I suspect to you also, though you may or may not have come to any steadfast conclusion, music (beauty) and God (Beauty) are the driving forces in your life. Do I equate God and music as One? To me I do – to you, that is your decision, of course.

I believe God (Father, Son and Holy Ghost) are all one – the embodiment of the best, the most lovely, the most beautiful, the highest and purest attainments possible in this human life – is the Creator, Sustainer, Ruler, Giver of all good and perfect gifts (nothing less). This is the God I worship.

Now, if my or your mental picture or spiritual understanding of God differs from each other, the preacher, the bishop, the drunk, the shop keeper or the Pope or Osama Bin Laden – so what? God is not so vain that he gives a fig about how we view Him – just so long as we search for the Good, the Perfect and the Beautiful.

This is a tough essay! I wish we could spend hours, days, nights sitting by the fireplace, drinking good brandy and discussing and searching our souls together. Perhaps that kind of spiritual depth is reserved for the life to come.

Love, Bob

(Of Acute Embarrassment)   (16 September 2007)

Dear Bob

I think the wisest thing I can do is change the subject. I don't recognise myself in your scenario!

I always found that music was ninety-nine per cent hard work and one per cent inspiration.

(On the Loss of Friends)   (10 October 2007)

Dear Ann,

I am writing through the tears that came as I read about your parents' last days. As you know from past writings, your father was a surrogate father to me, as well as the master musician I had as a role model. Your mother, though I, of course, saw much less of her, was the attractive older lady who played viola in the R.P.I. Orchestra, had perfect pitch and who winced at my lousy intonation (not often!) on the clarinet as we played Beethoven's *Pastorale Symphony*.

Ann, there are no words that don't seem trite at this point, other than I loved them and realize that each of us has our own personal demons to contend with.

The ache is when we have no choice other than to stand by, watch and cry. When death comes, no matter its shape or form, we do it alone – by ourselves. The loved ones stand and shed tears, but we die all by ourselves – it is our last triumphant act!

I went through the deaths of my former wife's parents, of whom I was very fond. Her father had emphysema which is a damnable disease. Her mother, my mother-in-law, died of meanness. Still, it was a difficult time.

Like you, I am sure, I find comfort and joy in the years Milton and Mary had in London after arriving there. Your father was a great talent who, it seems, found his bliss in the creation of music rather than the recognition and accolades that can accompany it. I understand and applaud that.

I should have liked so much to have been able to sit with him and argue violently the merits of Mozart vs Beethoven. We could have drunk coffee by the gallon and smoked cigarettes by the pack!

Back to the present (often a painful transition) – Ann, here we are, separated by miles of space and so together spiritually. We talk about our parents a generation back, and now we see ourselves as 'them'.

When I recall my own father, who was a brilliant and serene gentleman at age seventy-three (my age now), I recall a rather elderly gentleman who didn't get around as well as he once did, but was still just as quick of mind and wit. Could it be that that is how my kids see me? Likely.

I know what you mean when you say writing about this time is painful. It is painful for me to read, and I wasn't even a participant!

Much love, Bob

(More on Death)   (11 October 2007)

Dear Bob,

Having been near death several times, I have reached the conclusion that we die when our time comes; not sooner, not later. I had a high fever as a child, and I lived. I was run over by a car when in my early twenties, and I lived.

What I haven't told you about, my dear motorcycling friend, is the time I came off my bike in the middle lane of a motorway. As I mentioned earlier, I rode my motorcycle every weekend to visit my parents, keep them company and do whatever odd jobs they wanted. One day, as I was returning home, my motorcycle got picked up in crosswinds. The rear wheel was lifted completely off the tarmac. I can tell you, I was scared! It's surprising how heightened my senses were. In a split second, I knew I had to hang onto the bike as it turned over and let it drag me forward in a straight line; had I let go, I might have been thrown into the fastest lane, or I might have lost the forward momentum too soon and been run over by the car behind. But, incredibly, the driver of the car behind me saw what was happening, and he and the person in the slow lane pulled up their cars and stopped traffic in all but the fast lane. They put their cars at risk, but they saved my life. Thanks to their quick thinking, I wasn't hurt at all. The knees were ripped out of my motorcycle suit, but not out of my jeans underneath. I was unhurt.

I think I might call that a miracle.

When the policeman arrived (one of the drivers stayed with me until he appeared), I shocked this poor man by practically throwing myself at him. We had to wait ages for the rescue van to show up, and I knew my parents would be frantic if I didn't ring them at the usual time. Also, the policeman's shift ended while we waited, but he stayed with me anyway, and even arranged for someone to ring my parents to say I had broken down.

Love, Ann

THUMB THINGS
or
A Tale of Two Digits

(Of Memories and Fears)   (2 June 2005)

Dear Ann,

I remember one day at R.P.I when I was in your father's String class (a Music Education class). About twenty voice, woodwind, brass and percussion majors were sawing away in first position. There was a drummer in the class – he was a fine jazz drummer and an extremely large, muscular guy, but not vthe sharpest tool in the shed. On top of that, he was completely tone deaf. Your Dad stopped the group and in an exasperated voice said, "Burley (the drummer), what the Hell are you doing?" The class fell apart! I dropped Music Education and graduated in Performance. I think 'Fiddle Class' pushed me over the edge!

Ann, you said you have retired from the flute for 'health reasons'. Does that mean you never touch the flute, or just don't perform anymore? How do you cope or feel about that? I would be honoured to listen.

This is important to me because I face the grim reality of either hanging the flute up as a wall decoration, or my playing just deteriorating due to very painful arthritis in BOTH thumbs, as well as glaucoma which is making it increasing difficult to read music that isn't 'blown up' – sort of like the Roy Clark *Big Note Song Book.* Ledger lines really are a mess as they all run together so A2 and C3 etc. all look alike.

I guess this is not a very cheery mail, but it would be helpful to hear your thoughts on the flute and closing the case for the last time. Sometimes I think it would be less painful emotionally to quit playing while ahead and not suffer the agony of one's playing slowly going down the drain.

I have no concept of your feelings on your playing. You attained great heights as a flutist. I, on the other hand, never reached anything other than local and regional renown, which never bothered me. I played for myself. If someone else liked it, great – if not, too bad. Hanging the flute up would be very similar to saying goodbye to a beloved friend.

Enough of this as it is getting dismal!

(Slings and Arrows)   (10 June 2005)

Dear Bob

Is there some sort of splint that a physiotherapist could devise to reduce the weight of the flute, at least for your right hand? Physical therapy for stretching the left thumb and forefinger? I'll shut up – I'm sure you have already tried everything that's at all possible! I shall hope for the best for you.

I have Parkinson's disease. It has put period to flute playing. Maybe I don't mind that as much as you do. While I was occasionally brilliant (yes, yes, I admit it shamelessly!), I was not consistent. I might have played the socks off James Galway on one concert, but there was no guarantee that the next one would be as good. Teaching was what I really liked.

(Of bandages and Blisters) (6 August 2005)

Dear Ann

I am expected to play a gig in Lexington on Sunday, but I had a little accident with the lawnmower and burned my fingers quite badly. I have had to wrap them up in bandages. I hope they will recover in time!

(On Fortitude)   (August 2005)

Dear Bob

Thank God you just burned your fingers on the lawnmower! You might have cut them off! From what I know of you, your performance on Sunday will be stunning, blisters, bandages and all! I have a friend (former pupil) who is a little deformed – one side of her body is slightly bigger then the other half, though you don't really notice it. Also, one leg was amputated below the knee when she was a child. Her bones keep cracking and although she's only in her forties, she has had a hip replacement, a broken shoulder and numerous other problems. She played a concert once with the left side of her body in a cast from the foot to her waist. She had to stand the whole evening because she couldn't bend enough to sit down. She is not a lady who quits!

And you are not a man who quits. I have no doubt you will be stunning in Lexington!

(Giving Up The Flute, Part 1)   *(Undated)*

Dear Ann

Sorry I didn't get back to you sooner! The weekend gig in Lexington, VA, at Washington and Lee University went, though I am not sure where! That's about all I can say. Ann, I am at a loss as to how to cope with my thumbs. They are getting to be a real problem, especially when I try to play. I am scheduled to play this Sunday in church with the choir on a Buxtehude thing. I have concluded that the best thing for me to do after Sunday is retire from flute playing.

It took awhile and a lot of hurt to come to this conclusion, but I honestly think it is for the best. Maybe I can learn to play a trumpet or trombone as neither use thumbs!

Enough of my bellyaching! Let me know how YOU are and what is happening in your world.

(On Opportunity)   *(25 September 2005)*

Dear Bob

I hardly know what to say. It's a tough decision. I ache for you. When you are a little recovered from the pain of your decision, you will be able to see that you have many fine memories to enjoy. You have given joy and comfort through your music and you have helped and guided young talented players. You were blessed with musical ability and you have used this gift wisely. Musicians are special people. You can be proud of what you have done.

Now is the time to create a new future. Aren't you lucky! Few people have even one real chance in life.

With love and best wishes for an exciting new future.

(Playing Again)   *(27 September 2005)*

Dear Bob

That's good news! A chance to perform the Telemann *Suite*! If you can play that, there's nothing much wrong with your thumbs! Lovely music! When is the performance?

What a funny way you have of packing up the flute! I'm not listening to any more of your threats to quit playing. Every time you say you have quit, you haven't! I think you'll play 'til your toes turn up!!

And I like your stubbornness.

(On Nobility vs Ignobility) (14 December 2005)

Dear Bob

I lost the weight quite a while ago. It's only now that I'd like something more elegant to wear than jeans that it's causing problems. I weigh ninety-eight pounds. Do you remember the Atlas ads? 'Don't be a ninety-eight pound weakling.' I'm not. I'm ninety-eight pound heavy.

You want the raw truth about my putting the flute down. I wish I'd put it down sooner. My last three concerts were horrendous. I wish I had known at the time that I had PD, but I didn't. I was nonplussed to find I was playing so badly.

At least you know that your thumbs lock. You can leave on a high. I left on a downer. Only you can know if you want to quit while you're still able to play, or if you prefer to risk a bad performance. There's nothing noble about forcing yourself to perform as long as possible. Nor is there anything ignoble about quitting while you're ahead.

Perhaps you could make sure the audience is filled with friends who understand your problem. And have a student ready to stand in if you have to give up half way through the concert.

Sorry, Bob. It's a rotten decision. My heart is with you.

(Giving Up The Flute 2)   *(4 March 2006)*

Dear Ann

We had the worst orchestra rehearsal ever! I sat while the orchestra practised *Hansel and Gretel* (horrors) – then we spent fifteen minutes on Telemann, on two spots in the overture where the fiddles get lost. I played a total of no more than twenty notes and then we went home.

Is it worth getting up on Saturday and being ready to practise at 9am? I suppose you can tell I am somewhat down in the dumps over it. I have spent the afternoon eating jelly beans and writing about fifteen measures on flute and piano music.

(On the Avoidance of Shame)   (27 March 2006)

My dear, dear Bob,

Thank you for confiding in me.

It's a horrible decision to make. I'm so sorry! But I won't offer you pity, only sympathy. And that in its place.

I have been worrying about you a lot. I suspect – only you can know – that you have made the right decision. You have so much going for you and you have been suffering so much pain for so long! It's nicer to quit on an 'up', rather than a 'down'. Now you can enjoy your retirement without shame or embarrassment, and the memories will all be happy ones.

And you have enjoyed lots of wonderful rehearsals on the Telemann, and you won't have to worry about that cellist who can't read music!

And you have your composition and your mental health and family and friends.

(On Being Well-Oiled)   (2 June 2006)

Dear Bob

The visit with the kinesiologist went well. He smothered me in oils, one of which smelled like brandy, and I travelled home, reeking, on a very crowded (rush hour) tube. People would look at me and when I returned their looks, they would quickly turn away. Except for one little girl who kept trying to tell her mommy about me, and mommy was obviously embarrassed. Add to the brandy smell the fact that my balance is rather wobbly, and I must have looked like the worst kind of alcoholic! One day I will write a funny story about this.

(Of a weighty matter) *(10 June 2006)*

Dear Bob

The hypnotherapist can't make me do things like TV hypnotists seem to do to people. I hear everything he says (though I think this will change as I get used to it) and process it myself in a state of deep relaxation. He has been trying to increase my appetite – I weigh – should I say, last week and for several months before that, I weighed ninety-one pounds. I have added about five pounds to that in the last two weeks. He is doing research on using hypnosis to overcome incurable diseases, and I will become a case study. It's intensely interesting.

(Giving Up The Flute 3)   (16 August 2006)

Dear Ann

Well, the inevitable has finally arrived after many attempts to sidestep it. September 13 is the day my thumb surgery will take place. I simply cannot continue playing with this much discomfort.

(On Delayed Action)   (27 August 2006)

Dear Ann

I have a confession – I called the doctor and went over for a consultation and we cancelled the thumb surgery. He agreed with me that life would be impossible for me, (with no spousal support) to do the things I need to do while the hand was immobile. I am going for steroid shots (I will be the world's only flutist on steroids!). He said, in time (hopefully a long time) I would need the operation. At least now I can plan to play the sonatas that came over from the UK!

(On Glib Assumption)   *(31 August 2006)*

Dear Ann

I get my steroid shot at 3pm today – and have a 5pm flute rehearsal with my accompanist to resurrect the Telemann *F Major Sonata* to play for the Prelude Sunday. I never thought that maybe I won't be able to use my thumb that soon. 'Sweet Mystery of Life…' On top of that, we have a hurricane coming here by afternoon. Life is so exciting!!

I would like to thank you, dear Ann, for being in my life at this particular time.

(Giving Up The Flute 4)   *(10 November (2006)*

Dear Ann

I am doing surprisingly well with not playing. I lovingly packed the flute away and haven't seen it in three or four days. Not bad – I miss your emails more than playing... how's that for dedication?

(On Flutes and Sermons) *(11 November 2006)*

Dear Bob

I appreciate what a tough decision you are making. I don't think you should sell your flute yet!

No one but a musician understands this particular kind of hell. At least you have had the warmth of your flute for years, and it has always been there for you. Few people have been so rich.

Grieve for a while. Then get on with your life. Compose a major work. Share your knowledge by writing a treatise on music and sending it to a magazine. Do something entirely different – write a novel about musicians, or about your experiences joining music and religion. Take up photography. Or painting. Above all, remember that when one door closes, there are many other doors waiting to be opened.

End of sermon, preacher. You are with me in my thoughts.

(On popping pills)   *(29 November 2006)*

Dear Bob

The weather here is also ridiculously warm. A couple or three nights ago, it was quite cold and I thought winter had finally come – but it didn't last.

I had an appointment with the neurologist yesterday. He suggested giving me some more medication but I refused. I think I'm doing okay. The short period of pain has passed, and for all I know, it may not have been PD that caused it. I'm frightened of the medication, more than I am of the disease. I will increase it only when I have to.

(Playing Again)   *(13 December 2006)*

Dear Ann

Hey – I picked up the flute and spent about fifteen minutes on some wonderful little tone warm-ups of Galway's. Beautiful! I was so happy!!

Then I decided to work slowly on the easiest Bach Sonata (not easy – just eas*ier*) ... Number 4 in C. Well, after a few minutes of the C Scale in 1/16ths, I had to stop and soak my hands in hot water. My enthusiasm exceeds reality, I think.

(On Operations)   (4 January 2007)

Dear Ann

The thumb doctor scheduled surgery for February 2. I am going to follow through this time. There is nothing to lose. As it is, the flute is out of the question; I haven't had it out of the case since October! So on February 2, I shall enter the hospital as an outpatient with great exuberance and hopeful for a new thumb! You will accompany me there in my heart.

The surgeon's office just called and had to reschedule my little surgery for February 16 instead of February 2. No problem. No, not both thumbs this time. The right thumb and if it works well, I will do the left one later on.

The operation was postponed since the surgeon found out he had to be away on a seminar or something. I have come thus far, another two weeks won't matter. I haven't had the flute out the case now since the end of October. I'd rather never play again than have the pain and hear such horribly uneven scale passages emit from the end of the flute. Hopefully, all that will be fixed shortly.

(On Turtles and Sloths)   *(16 February 2007)*

Dear Ann

It's done! I am home, everything went fine, now all I have to do is recuperate. The right hand is totally numb. I have a high-powered pain killer, but I hope I won't need it as the side effects are dangerous.

I am finding out what life would be like doing all of life's necessities with no right hand. Slow but, like the proverbial turtle, sure. I go to the doctor next Friday to have it checked, and I hope reduce the size of the cast.

I got a call last night from the choir director. His father had a serious stroke yesterday, and he asked me to direct the choir on Sunday. I had no choice as the poor man has to travel two hundred miles to be with his father in the hospital.

So, if you can, imagine a choral director using, rather than a baton, a plaster cast to lead the choir? It should be interesting!

(Time and CASTaways)   *(5 March 2007)*

Dear Ann

The cast came off Friday, as did the stitches. My arm looks hideous. The doctor gave (sold!) me a brace that I can remove when I want. If I leave it off too long, my hand begins to pain me. I think I keep it on about a third of the time.

My thumb is doing very nicely. In fact, I keep the brace off seventy-five per cent of the time. Every so often I forget, and move it in a direction it won't go – and that can at times be painful. According to my doctor, it takes two months to get completely healed. So by April 16, I should be as good as new. I still have patiently not tried the flute as I want to make a pain free trial to see if the low keys can be played at all – and can be played without pain. Time will tell.

(Of Facts and Confidence)   (13 March 2007)

Dear Ann

I am getting a bit out of sorts with my hand. It hurts with a different kind of pain in a different spot. I am so worried about playing. Technique is not my forte, I have to work on each and every rapid passage. If my body works against me, it will just be a sad thing indeed. I will stop being morose.

I have practised a bit now for two days, and it went as well as I could have expected. The tone, technique, intonation, breath control, timbre and memory are pretty fuzzy!

I did have a little pain, more as I played awhile. I am confident I can make a comeback. At least, I will give it my best effort.

(Giving Up the Flute 5)   *(undated)*

Dear Bob
I'm sorry you are selling your flute.
Now put your talents to work re-learning the trumpet. Or buy yourself a drum kit and drive the neighbours mad. And remember, I am with you in spirit.
Much love, Ann

Richmond String Quartet
Milton Cherry, Henry Liscio, Donald Tennant, Mary Cherry

Mary and Milton Cherry in period dress
for a concert series at the Virginia Museum

Milton Cherry puts daughter Ann on a plane to Italy

Wigmore Hall
WIGMORE STREET, W.1
Manager: William Lyne

WEDNESDAY
14th JANUARY 1970
at 7.30 p.m.

ANN CHERRY   Flute
BERNARD KING   Piano

This concert is sponsored by The Music and Drama Club of Cleveland, Ohio

Concert Management: **WILFRID VAN WYCK LTD.**

Tickets: **12/6** **8/6** **5/-**

Obtainable from the Wigmore Hall Box Office (Tel: 01-935 2141): Weekdays 10-8, Saturdays 10-12.30 and usual Agents
Please enclose stamped addressed envelope with postal applications

Programme Overleaf

Flyers for Ann Cherry's debut in the Wigmore Hall, London

Bob says, "Here is the first band I ever played with in high school. I was fifteen. I am the dopey one in the back – 1947." behind the saxophones.

I found this one of the 7th Army Band in Stuttgart in the city concert hall. I am the pudgy one playing piccolo (eek) on the very end of the first row.

I look like a child. I was a child.
I like being a man much better.
1957 Senior Recital.

Bob's children, Lillian and Tommy, in 1966.

Bob's concert at St Thomas, Savannah, Georgia, 1981

Here I am in my alter-ego outfit!

A band I was in played New Year's Eve in Hilton Head, NC in 1996.

This 1986 pic is me on my
BMW motorcycle stopping for a smoke